PENGUIN PLAYS

PL26

THE DREAM OF PETER MANN

BERNARD KOPS

THE DREAM
OF PETER MANN

BY BERNARD KOPS

—

WITH AN INTRODUCTION BY
MERVYN JONES

PENGUIN BOOKS

Penguin Books Ltd, Harmondsworth, Middlesex
U.S.A.: Penguin Books Inc., 3300 Clipper Mill Road, Baltimore 11, Md
AUSTRALIA: Penguin Books Pty Ltd, 762 Whitehorse Road,
Mitcham, Victoria

—

First published 1960

—

Copyright © Bernard Kops, 1960

Made and printed in Great Britain
by Unwin Brothers Limited
Woking and London

FOR ERICA MY LOVE
AND FRANK MY FRIEND

*With thanks to
The Arts Council under whose bursary
this play was written*

CONTENTS

INTRODUCTION

IT is hard to say which piece of news is the best: that Bernard Kops should have written this remarkable play, that it should be produced, or that it should be published in a popular edition. All three events are signs of the extraordinary and unlooked-for rejuvenation of the English theatre that is still quickening its pace.

Five years ago, we had what was politely known as 'an actor's theatre'. That is to say, standards of production and performance had reached a peak of unenterprising perfection, displayed either in plays of mournful triviality or in ornamented revivals of the classics. A new play, by definition, was a play from France or the United States. Penguin Books could not have published a volume – much less a series – of New English Dramatists, because there were none. The very few who laid claim to this description were hastily shouldered into the wings amid a rhubarb-sound of shocked murmurs, as if someone had started to play a guitar in a cathedral.

Now we have a whole string of young, vigorous, genuinely important playwrights; and the best thing about them is that they are not a string, or a group, or a school. Each has his own voice and his own vision. *The Dream of Peter Mann* is an original work in the truest sense. It is by virtue of its originality that it takes a natural place in the new drama.

Shaftesbury Avenue, of course, is the last place to hear of anything new in the theatre. Of the writers who matter today, all must go to Wyndham's by way of Wigan Pier. Bernard Kops' route has been especially circuitous. Penguin buyers will have recognized the quality of his first play, *The Hamlet of Stepney Green*, published in the first volume of *New English Dramatists*; it was produced in Germany, Holland, and the United States – and at the Oxford Playhouse. *Change for the Angel* came to the Arts Theatre. *The Dream of Peter Mann* made its bow at the Edinburgh Festival, which is about the only affinity between Bernard Kops and T. S. Eliot.

The people you will meet in this play are not 'ordinary people', because, to a writer of any talent, the world is populated by two billion unique individuals. However, they are people living in ordinary circumstances in the Britain of 1960. Bernard Kops does not write with conscious effort 'about the working-class'; he writes naturally about, and for, people who queue for buses and not people who hail taxis, people who buy from stalls and not people who maintain charge accounts. Almost casually, he and the other new dramatists have made the Mayfair drawing-rooms into what the solemnly proletarian settings of the 1930s too often seemed: a curious corner of British life.

Call this realism if you like; but it is realism employed as M. Jourdain used prose. Using the language of reality, the imagination is ardently at work, and the result has the truth of art, which is a deeper truth than mere verisimilitude. No social survey of Salford will discover the odd ménage of *A Taste of Honey*, and the eavesdropper in a Norfolk cottage will wait a long time to overhear a scene like the third act of *Roots*. Similarly, shopkeepers in the streets of our cities do not say the things they say in *The Dream* (or even outside the dream) *of Peter Mann*. Bernard Kops is there to help them say these things. This is why he employs a dialogue that, although colloquial and authentic, gains a heightened eloquence from its powerfully marked rhythm, extended at times – and this is among the most facinating of Kops' techniques – by the use of song.

He also makes use of a convention which will be accepted easily and even unconsciously by those who see the play, but which should perhaps be mentioned to readers of a printed text. It is fully as legitimate as any of Shakespeare's conventions and a good deal less awkward than some. His characters put into words feelings and ideas which, in strict realism, they could not express and might not even know about. If we ignore this, the lines appear ruthless and sentimental by turns. But the truth is that we live our lives without admitting our capacity either for harshness or for love.

This is a play of bold ambition, which enormously extends the dimensions of common life. The large forces that mould or menace our world are made to impinge directly on the characters. As in some other recent plays, people speak of the hydrogen bomb. Real people, maybe, don't do this except at political meetings, but they feel continually the presence of the bomb. Kops has given them words for that feeling, and the open-eyed courage to face and overcome it. This is not a play 'about' the bomb; it is a play about living in a world that has the bomb.

There is another reality, more central to the play, which we commonly ignore even for a lifetime and of which these characters are made painfully but triumphantly aware. A curtain of incomprehension, thickened by pretence, divides one real self from another. Early in the play, Peter Mann says to the girl he wants to marry: 'Isn't that strange, we've lived here all our lives together and now we're strangers.' How many young men and girls do in fact get married without ever daring to say or even to think that? In plays by some of the new dramatists, the persistence of this barrier is a theme for tragedy. In others, the drama derives from a difficult and unresolved struggle against it. But in *The Dream of Peter Mann* the break-through is ultimately effected, giving at the end a justly earned sense of exaltation. By this the play stands or falls, and I think it stands as a wholly satisfying work of art.

For, despite its candid portrayal at the necessary moments of misery and terror, this is finally a joyous play and an affirmation of the love of life. The quality of this affirmation is often realized through humour. This humour is never a diversion, a whistling in the dark, an attempt to shrug off unpleasant truths. On the contrary, these very truths are faced and illuminated by humour. As G. K. Chesterton said, all the really good jokes are about serious things.

What, after all, is life when we experience it to the full? Let Peter Mann answer: 'The one and only – all shapes and sizes – lovely, lousy, terrible, terrific. Magnificent! Ridiculous! But it's the only one we've got. A great opportunity never to be repeated – a unique bargain – going – going – so make the most of it before it's gone!'

That is the real theme of every genuine artist, and he is measured by his understanding of it and his success in rendering it. It is by these high standards that Bernard Kops' play asks to be judged.

MERVYN JONES

THE DREAM OF PETER MANN

Presented by Lynoq Productions at the Edinburgh Festival 1960
First performance 5 September 1960 at the Lyceum Theatre
Directed by Frank Dunlop
Décor by Richard Negri
Music by Ricet-Barrier

CHARACTERS OF THE PLAY

ALEX, *a tramp*

MR GREEN, *a greengrocer*

MRS GREEN, *the wife of the greengrocer*

PETER MANN, *a dreamer*

MAN (MR SMALL), *a worker*

MR BUTCHER, *a butcher*

MR FISH, *a fishmonger*

MRS BUTCHER, *the wife of the butcher*

MRS FISH, *the wife of the fishmonger*

SYLVIA, *daughter of Mr and Mrs Green*

JASON, *an undertaker*

SONIA MANN, *proprietress of the gown shop*

PENNY, *daughter of Mr and Mrs Butcher*

TOM GROOM, *a prospective bridegroom of Penny*

JOHN

JACK

ACT ONE

The scene is a market-place in London.

Several market stalls are standing empty outside several closed shops. These are: a Butcher's shop, a Greengrocer's, a Fishmonger's, a Gown shop, and an Undertaker's.

The stalls are used as accessory to the shops, and it is from these that most of the goods are sold.

Each shop has an appropriate sign painted above it. The undertaker's sign simply says 'Twenty-Four-Hour Service'.

The gown shop is the largest and has a large shutter with a door in it. Gowns and rolls of material are all around the shop.

Time is the present. It is a beautiful mid-summer morning, and the stage is deserted.

> [*Some children are heard singing, then activity begins. One by one the shops are opened; goods are brought out and displayed on the stalls. The gown shop remains closed.*]

CHILDREN [*voices off*]: Peach, Plum, or Apricot!
　　　　　How much money have you got?
　　　　　If you've got a bob or two,
　　　　　I will bring some home for you.

> [SYLVIA *enters from the shop of* MR AND MRS GREEN. *Her arms are full of flowers. She arranges them on her stall which stands outside the undertaker's shop.*]

CHILDREN [*voices off*]: Apricot, Peach, or Plum!
　　　　　We may get blown to kingdom come.
　　　　　Let us eat our fruit before
　　　　　Our parents go again to war.

> [ALEX *enters, a ragged tramp, with a swagger of dignity. He goes to the fruit stall.*]

ALEX: I would like a pound of plums.

MR GREEN: Certainly, sir. [*Weighs them.*]

ALEX: I only wish I had the money to pay for them.

MR GREEN: Clever bloke – aren't you – get away from my stall.

MRS GREEN: What's the world coming to – it's full of lousy good-for-nothings.

[ALEX *bows; as he walks away from the stall he relishes a peach that he has stolen. As the children sing he takes a great bite.*]

CHILDREN [*voices off*]: Plum, Apricot, or Peach,
        Hide the stone from out their reach,
        So that it falls into the earth,
        And brings another world to birth.

[ALEX *wanders around, smells the flowers, and is amused by what he sees. All the traders rush around. The* BUTCHER *is dressed in evening dress and his wife in a long evening gown. He plucks a chicken and smokes a cigar.* ALEX *sits down on the pavement outside the gown shop, takes out a pocket chess set, and plays a game of chess with himself. The shutter of the gown shop is thrown open and* PETER *emerges, yawning.*]

PETER: Good morning morning! Another blinking day.

[PETER *starts to bring out rolls of cloth but in the middle of this he sees* ALEX.]

PETER: Playing chess? I'll give you a game.

ALEX: Not on your Nelly – I only play against myself. This way I can cheat to my heart's content and I never lose.

PETER: They say there's more out than in.

[*He returns to his stall. A man enters carrying an umbrella and wearing glasses.*]

MAN [*to* MR BUTCHER *who is pulling a chicken*]: Please can I have a tasty, ready for the plate, oven fresh, delicious chicken pie?

MR BUTCHER: What did you say?

MAN: Can I have an oven fresh, chilled, ready cooked chicken pie?

MR BUTCHER [*brandishing knife*]: Get out of my shop before I mince you.

MAN [*going to* MR FISH]: Don't they want customers?

MR FISH: Can I help you? Lovely haddock? Beautiful flaky cod?

16

Whiting? Fresh water trout? Beautiful Scotch salmon? Just been landed out of the sea.

MAN: Fish? Yes! I would like, let me see – [*Consults note*.] Ah yes, a packet of frozen, ready prepared, and absolutely succulent, hygienically-sealed fish fingers, please.

MR FISH: Did I hear you right?

MAN: You should move with the times.

MR FISH: I'll move you, you little eel.

MAN [*rushing to* MR GREEN]: What's the matter with everyone here? They are all mad.

MR GREEN: Lettuces are crisp today and radishes are juicy. Aubergines are lovely, mauve and sweet. Green peppers are hot and artichokes are cheap and fresh. What do you want? Some bananas? Oranges? Apples? Lemons? Nuts? Cabbages? Sprouts? Lovely fresh peas?

MAN: Peas? Yes please. A packet of frozen peas, please.

MR GREEN: Would you mind repeating that?

MAN: Packed foods save time.

MR GREEN: Time for what?

MAN: Why, time for – time for – what? Time for time of course. Now you're driving me as mad as yourself. Don't you see we haven't got time, that's why we live out of tins. You're all living in the past, everyone buys at the Superstores, that's why this market's dead.

PETER: That's what I told them. Join together, make more money.

MR GREEN: ⎤ All you make is trouble.

MRS BUTCHER: ⎬ You're a snotty-nosed big mouth.

MRS FISH: ⎦ Too big for your boots, that's your trouble.

MRS BUTCHER: ⎤ If I was your Mum I'd smack your bum and send you packing. [*To husband*] It's time you stood up to him, he insults me and you do nothing.

MRS GREEN [*to husband*]: We ought to get up a petition. He ought to be abolished. Can't you do something about it?

MRS FISH [*to husband*]: He's a mischief-maker. Please, move yourself, get rid of him.

MR BUTCHER: Well, I may be a weak-kneed, pigeon-livered, hen-pecked has been –

MR FISH: } Ditto.
MR GREEN: } Ditto.

MR BUTCHER: But now I've made up my mind and I'm determined to do something.

MR GREEN: } So am I.
MR FISH: } So am I.

MRS BUTCHER: About time, too. What are you going to do?

MR BUTCHER: I'm going to put my foot down and tell you to go to hell.

MR FISH: } Same here.
MR GREEN: } Me too.

MR BUTCHER: Apart from that, I'm going to do nothing; so leave me alone and give me a bit of peace.

MR GREEN: } You said it. That's telling them.
MR FISH: } That's certainly telling them. [*They continue working slowly.*]

MAN: I know just how you feel. I get up in the morning, wife's asleep. From a tin of milk and a tin of coffee I make myself a tin mug of tea – Well, it tastes the same – From the refined wheat-free waxed wrapped loaf I make some sandwiches using tinned corned beef. I rush to work in a tin train, packed like sardines, and in the tin factory I make tincans all day. When I come home, my wife opens a tin of baked beans and stewed steak. I follow her to bed. She lies beside me like a cold chicken pie ready for the oven but I am too exhausted and fall asleep. I dream of tins and tins and tins and tens of thousands of tins and nightmares of tin horses and I wake up screaming, 'Help, help, I've lost the opener'.

MR GREEN: Why don't you make a stand?

MAN: You trying to make me discontented? I shall never come to this market again. [*He is about to stomp off when he sees the flower stall.*] A carnation, please.

SYLVIA: Certainly, sir. [*She fixes one in his buttonhole.*]

MAN: Wish it was a reincarnation.

SYLVIA: Sorry, sir, we don't stock those.

JASON: I have a nice line in tin coffins that would suit you down to the ground.

[*Everyone laughs except the* MAN, *who stomps off.*]

ALEX: Checkmate! [*He stops playing and goes to* PETER.] *Could you* spare me a fag? [PETER *gives him one.*] Got a light? [PETER *lights it.*] Could you spare me a couple of bob? I'm down on my luck this week.

PETER [*giving him money*]: Now get out of my life, I've got enough worries.

ALEX: Perhaps I can help you, sonny?

[PETER *pushes him to one side and sadly goes to* SYLVIA *who pretends to ignore him.* ALEX *follows* PETER.]

PETER: Forgive me for last night. I got carried away.

SYLVIA: Go away.

ALEX: Ah, forgive him, he really is sorry.

MR GREEN: He's talking to Sylvia again. How many times must I tell her the facts of life? He's no good. [*He rushes over to* PETER.] Now you stay away from my girl.

PETER: Pipe down. [MR GREEN *is afraid and rushes back to his wife.*]

MRS GREEN: Well, his mother's got pots of money, our daughter could do a lot worse.

MR GREEN: Before he was no good, but now you remember the money he's got and he's all right again.

MRS GREEN: Shut up and get on with your work.

ALEX: Leave this to me, son, I'll handle it.

PETER: I'll settle my own affairs.

MR GREEN: Did you hear that? They're having an affair.

MRS GREEN: Shut up.

PETER [*to* ALEX]: Now out of my way.

ALEX [*leans against the flower stall, between them, and takes a large flower, chrysanthemum, and starts plucking the petals, one by one*]: She loves him not, she loves him, she loves him not – [*Soon he is just mouthing the words.*]

SYLVIA: This a friend of yours?

PETER: Never seen him before in my life.

SYLVIA: Birds of a feather.

PETER: Sylvia, listen to me. I dreamed of you last night and the night before. I dream of you all the time. I love you.

ALEX: She loves him?

SYLVIA [to PETER]: Go away.

ALEX: Not!

PETER: Give me a chance.

SYLVIA: I gave you one once.

PETER: Give me another chance. I want to kiss you. You know you love me. [He tries to grab her; she pushes him off.]

SYLVIA: I know nothing of the kind.

PETER: Let's fly away together.

SYLVIA: I want a home.

PETER: I'll build one for you.

SYLVIA: What, with dreams? I want a boy with his feet on the ground.

PETER: Mine are! Mine are!

SYLVIA: My man must have his head screwed on.

PETER [shaking his head madly]: Mine isn't exactly falling off.

SYLVIA: I want to understand you but it's no use. If you give up your crazy ideas I'll be pleased to reconsider you. I'm a respectable girl and I need to settle down.

PETER: You once said you loved me. Down by the river, remember? And in the roundabout at Hampstead Heath and in the tube near Oxford Circus.

SYLVIA: You've changed. You were always so quiet; you were such a steady boy with your nose to the grindstone. When you swung the hammer the bell always rang.

PETER: How beautiful you are, lovelier than any flower. Throw away your flowers and come with me. Vision of purity, bloom of innocence.

SYLVIA: You're blooming daft.

PETER: Daft with love. Isn't that strange, we've lived here all our lives together and now we're strangers.

SYLVIA: You're beyond me.

PETER [*tries cuddling her again*]: I'll make you a queen. What do you want? Tell me.

SYLVIA: I want what every girl wants. To be courted slowly with chocolates. I want a lovely engagement ring, big and sparkling. I want everything planned. To be married in white and with flowers and bridesmaids. A choral wedding with everyone crying. I want to be pure on my wedding night. You're too impatient.

PETER: I'm normal. [*She fusses with flowers.*]

ALEX [*with the last handful of petals, throwing them away*]: She loves him not.

PETER: Women! They make me sick.

ALEX: I was married once; you can't tell me anything about women.

PETER: I'll show her. She'll change her mind one day and then she'll beg me to marry her. Guess what I'll do?

ALEX: What?

PETER: Marry her, of course. Oh, I wish I could leave.

ALEX: Wish I could settle down.

PETER: I'm shut in here.

ALEX [*lost in his own dream*]: 'Cos I'm not getting any younger.

PETER: I want money, sure, like the others, but I want something more.

ALEX: The nights get colder.

PETER: I don't get on with the yobs round here. I think of the future.

ALEX: I'm lonely.

PETER: I want to be stinking rich, open the most super-colossal Superstore you ever saw. If only I had the courage to just go.

ALEX: Come with me.

PETER: That's not a bad idea. Do you mean it?

ALEX: Sure. I'll show you the ropes.

[*They laugh and shake hands heartily.*]

PETER: I'll have my fling with every so and so and reap my wild sluts. [*He jumps on to the stall.*] Girls of the world. Hear me. Dolls, damsels, virgins, skirts, floozies, listen to me! I'm coming your way, don't get impatient! I've got time for all of you. Casanova, Don

Juan, Yul Brynner, stand to one side: Mann is coming to show you how to make love. Girls! Stop crying for me, stop chewing your pillow cases, take down those photos, I'm coming in the flesh to make *your* flesh tingle. It'll be the thrill of a lifetime.

ALEX: Hip! Hip! Hoor . . .

[ALEX *applauds but it falls on silence and all in the market shake their heads.*]

ALEX: Come on, let's go.

PETER [*jumping down*]: Sorry, I'd like to but I can't.

ALEX: Why not?

PETER: All the mountains have been climbed, all the deserts have been crossed and all the records smashed.

ALEX: Got a fag?

PETER [*gives him one.* ALEX *pockets it*]: There's nothing for me to do but get old and fat and pass on the business to my horrible kids. There's nothing worth living for and nothing worth dying for. I'm fed up. Why did you have to come and make me unhappy?

ALEX: What, me?

[PETER *brings out rolls of material from the shop and displays them.* JASON *notices* ALEX *and stands close, considering him for something. Meanwhile –*]

MR BUTCHER [*to wife*]: When will they come home?

MRS BUTCHER: Stop worrying and clean those chickens.

MR BUTCHER: My own daughter gets married and you won't even let us take the day off.

MRS BUTCHER: We're essential workers. If we closed they'd all become anaemic or vegetarian or worse.

MR BUTCHER: What could be worse? Are we inviting them all to have a drink? [*He indicates the market people.*]

MRS BUTCHER: That means more expense. Oh, well.

MR BUTCHER: We must have some celebration, now we're dressed up like this.

MRS BUTCHER: Maybe, we'll see. Just get on with your work.

MR BUTCHER [*reading from a newspaper*]: It says that the fallout from one hydrogen bomb will kill ten million people. Some fallout.

MRS BUTCHER: Listen, when you get our age, the only fallout that should worry you should be your teeth and your hair. Don't yap so much, we have a very busy day.

JASON [*to* ALEX]: Excuse me, I couldn't help overhearing your conversation. How would you like to earn a fiver?

ALEX: Whose throat do I have to cut?

JASON: Just get rid of that young man.

ALEX: How?

JASON: Spin him a yarn, a tall story. Get him away from here. As far as possible.

ALEX: Why?

JASON: He's driving us all dotty.

ALEX [*taking money*]: All right, you talked me into it.

JASON: Incidentally, can I interest you in a life insurance policy? Down payment, one fiver.

ALEX: Who'd collect?

JASON: I am also local agent for the never-never furniture company, a qualified midwife, a marriage broker, and an undertaker. Jason is at your service from the cradle to the grave. And between you and me, as soon as Peter's out of the way I'm going into the gown industry by marrying his mother. Thank you, good day.

ALEX [*happily wanders to Peter's stall*]: Haven't had a pair of new socks since the Coronation. I'll treat myself. [*To* PETER] A pair of socks.

PETER: Show us the colour of your money. Good. Let's see what I can do you for. Now, these socks were made for the King of Egypt but because you're a punter they're going to you. [ALEX *takes his old socks off and puts the new pair on.*] Now I've only got fifty pairs left – step right up – Phew – [*he holds his nose.*]

ALEX: What about a shirt?

[PETER *gets a shirt and holds it like a bullfighter would his cloak. He fans the air with it, then he tries it on* ALEX.]

PETER: We've got the best shirts in the world. Shirts from the finest silk hot from first-grade cockney silkworms. Shirts for mere cash from Kashmir. [*Sings.*] Pale hands I love beside the Gaswork wall. – Flannel from the Channel, Cretonne for Cretins! Come on, step right up you silly sods, get your crappy crêpe here. [*The new shirt is much too big for Alex, but* PETER, *by pinching it in, makes it appear a perfect fit.*] There you are, a perfect fit!

ALEX: You're a very good salesman.

PETER: I would be if there were some customers. When a market goes down there's nothing you can do about it. Once upon a time my spiel left them spellbound but where are they? Look at it, Nylon Négligées, Lingering Lingerie, Beautiful Brassières, Combinations, Pants, and Petticoats and yards and yards of cloth all waiting for the moth. I feel useless.

ALEX: Nonsense. You've got imagination, you can go a long way. Especially North and South. That's where you'll find it.

PETER: What?

ALEX: Gold. In the Yukon.

PETER: Don't be crazy – you're fifty years late.

ALEX: Well, not exactly gold. Something better. Uranium!

PETER: Uranium? Where?

ALEX: Tons of it, mountains of it, handfuls of it. I'll take you to it.

PETER: They've got Geiger counters at the surplus store.

ALEX: We'll go North and stake a claim. The great uranium fever is sweeping the world. We can't wait to blow ourselves to smithereens.

PETER: Sounds terrific. [*He dances around the stage and then shouts at* ALEX] U – R –

ALEX: I am?

PETER: U – R – A –

ALEX: I am a what?

PETER: U – R – A – N – I – U – M – URANIUM!

[*He claps his hands and dances around from one stall to another.*]

PETER: Uranium, uranium, boom, boom, boom. [*They shake their heads and now he dashes to the flower stall where he sings to the indifferent* SYLVIA] Big bang bong bang – boom – womb – zoom – Get this in your cranium, stuff your old geranium, I'm off to find uranium – boom – boom – boom.

ALEX [*patting* PETER *on the back*]: That's my boy. We'll go just as we are. All we need is that Geiger counter and a little cash and we're in business.

PETER: How much money?

ALEX: How much you got? [PETER *doesn't reply.*] That's enough. Almost.

PETER: We'll make a fortune and I'll come back and buy up everything. I'll open the biggest, most fabulous Superstore and everyone will work for me. Great conditions! Five months' paid holiday a year, three-day week, sun lounge, hospitals, clocking-in machines ringing a hymn, like churchbells. URANIUM! My friend, we're in business. [*He sees* SONIA *coming out of the shop singing* 'Ochi Chornya, Ochi krasnya'.] Almost.

ALEX: Who's she?

PETER: My mother.

ALEX: Isn't she fat!

PETER: You said it. I'm sure one day she'll just float away.

[ALEX *buys some fruit and eats it.* JASON *goes to* SONIA *and puts his arm round her waist. She throws it off with virginal indignation.*]

SONIA [*to* JASON, *as he walks away*]: You're soon put off.

PETER: Listen folks, I'm about to leave you.

SONIA: Come here.

PETER: I've got the urge to go.

ALL: Hurray!

PETER: But I'll be back.

ALL: Ohhhhhhhh!

PETER: And I'll break your chains and set you free.

JASON: Sonia, what's he talking about?

SONIA: Mind your own business. Peter! What are you talking about.

PETER: U.R. – U.R.A. – U.R.A.N.I.U.M.

SONIA: I've got news for you. You're going mad, you madman. Now come down, do you hear?

PETER: This is Peter Mann the Uranium King – I'm on my way.

SONIA: Ooh! If you don't come here I shall die, I shall faint, I shall scream.

[*He dances in and out of shops embracing fruit and vegetables and chickens; he finally ends up kissing a cod.*]

PETER [*sings to tune of 'Serenade in the Night'*]: Farewell, little fish, my most passionate lover. Though I love you so – Now I really must go – in search of another – I've made up my mind, I'm going.

SONIA: You're out of your mind. You're not. Where?

PETER: Away.

SONIA: Why? Haven't you got everything you want?

PETER: Yes, but I want something more.

SONIA: Don't you love me?

PETER: Yes.

SONIA: Well, then, if you need a few extra pounds, just ask me. Shall we go away to Brighton for a few days?

PETER: No. Look, Mum, I want to go alone and come back rich.

SONIA: But you're rich now.

PETER: I never see money.

SONIA: I'm keeping it for a rainy day. It's in the safe, safe and sound.

PETER: You are an old miser.

SONIA: Don't I feed you? Don't I give you everything you want? Pineapple and cream and chicken and cheesecake – everything he wants.

PETER: Sorry, Mum, but I've got to go.

SONIA: It's in the blood. I knew it. Shall I remind you how I slaved for you, how I brought you up?

PETER: You've told me a thousand times.

SONIA: Oh, Peter –

PETER: Here we go again.

SONIA: What a beautiful child you were. [PETER *now mouths her words and apes her expressions.*] The things I did for you. Everything I sacrificed to make you happy and safe. I won't talk about your father, but you, you were the apple of my eye, so I left the old country on my own; that takes some doing, eh? A woman starting life again all on her own, and I was pregnant, seven months gone. I remember the journey on that boat.

PETER: I've heard this so many times before.

SONIA: Don't interrupt. You were just a bump inside me, hanging over the rail of that ship – did you kick! So I landed seven months pregnant; know what I did?

PETER: Yes.

SONIA: No, you don't. I hadn't a bean so I scrubbed floors and didn't understand a word of the language, and then you were born – with all that carbolic and brooms and mops, your big black eyes and soft curly hair.

PETER: Please pipe down.

SONIA: You were so beautiful. Any customers yet this morning?

PETER: Just one. This market's dead.

SONIA: How much have you taken?

PETER: A pound.

SONIA: Is that all? How dare you tell me such bad news? I think I'm going to have a stroke.

PETER: At the third stroke the time will be time I left. She's been on the verge of this stroke for fifteen years. Mum, thanks for everything but I'm really going. Just give me your blessing and a few quid.

SONIA: What do you want for lunch, Peter darling? A bit of roast chicken? Some boiled salmon?

PETER: It's no good, Mum. I want to find myself, I want to find love. [*Points to* SYLVIA.] And she won't have me.

SONIA: Only a mother could love you. No one else would have the patience or the insanity; anyway, darling, you're too good for her. That's the trouble – you're too good for anyone and I'm too good for you. [*She prepares to pretend to weep.*] Stop making me cry – my eyeblack will run. [*She sobs a bit, then when that doesn't work speaks again.*] Look, Peter darling, what are these fires raging in your head? Have a nice, cool lemonade and put them out. No more talking. Now run along, there's a good boy; take these pieces of cloth to Miller's warehouse, and yesterday's money to the bank.

[PETER *takes the money from her and takes several lengths of cloth.* JASON *goes to* SONIA.]

ALEX: We all set now? You ready?

27

PETER: First I've got to go on an errand. Carry these. [*He gives* ALEX *the cloth.*] This is the most beautiful blue, it's going-away blue.

ALEX: Blue is blue.

PETER: No, blue is for the seas and for the sky, for steel and smoke. And yellow, just look at this yellow.

ALEX: Yellow is for jaundice.

PETER: No, yellow is for deserts and for the cornfields, for spring flowers and lemons and sunshine. Yellow is for life. Don't you see? Every colour leads you somewhere, every colour is a country, every shade is a place, every piece of fruit, every flower, every fish, everything in this market tells me to go and find something, to find myself.

ALEX: You're right, blue is more than blue, yellow is more than yellow.

PETER: And I'm more than I am. Let's go – by the way, what's your name?

ALEX: Alex. [*They shake hands.*] What have you got in your hand?

PETER: Money.

ALEX: Let me carry it.

PETER: No.

ALEX: Don't you trust your best friend?

PETER: Sure, but not as far as money's concerned.

ALEX: Look, you've got everything because you've got imagination. You're the richest person I know – it would be a pity to get all clogged up with money. I'm down to earth, let me arrange the sordid details. [*He dances around* PETER *and covers the boy with the cloth which* PETER *unwinds and rewinds as they dance together.*]

ALEX [*sings*]: Hi! Hi! Dance and sing, money doesn't mean a thing. You must give it all to me if you want the golden key. Hi! Hi! Sing and shout, it's time to throw your money out, if you throw it in my purse – I'll give you the Universe. [PETER *gives* ALEX *the money.*] Hi! Hi! Dance for joy, the spinning world is now your toy – and you'll become the greatest King for money doesn't mean a thing. [*They laugh.*]

SONIA: Who is that man dancing with Peter?

JASON: Just a tramp.

SONIA: I thought so; he has a shifty face.

JASON: Peter will be safe with him, I'm sure.

SONIA: I hope so. He's such a good boy.

JASON: I wonder, though, if he'll be safe with Peter?

SONIA: What did you say?

JASON: I said I have business to discuss with you later.

SONIA: As long as it's not monkey business.

PETER ⎱ [they dance off together, singing]: Hi, Hi, dance and sing,
ALEX ⎰ money doesn't mean a thing – not much! [They exit.]

MRS BUTCHER [to MR BUTCHER]: All right, if you must you can tell them now.

MR BUTCHER: Friends! As you know, my daughter, Penny, is being married. They'll be back from the church shortly and we want you all to have a drink with us.

MRS BUTCHER: More expense. I don't know – oh well, it might have been worse. What a lucky escape I've had. That madman Peter Mann could have been my son-in-law.

MRS FISH: That was a lucky escape.

MR BUTCHER: So we'll all forget work for a few hours and enjoy ourselves. What about it? [Silence as people carry on working.] A change is – as good – as a rest – ? A few drinks? – you're only – young once? What's the world coming to?

SYLVIA [goes to them]: Would you like to buy some flowers?

MR BUTCHER: Certainly dear. Some lilies for purity.

SYLVIA: That's a laugh.

MRS BUTCHER: Well, Sylvia dear, you'd better hurry up. My Penny's beaten you to the bedpost.

SYLVIA: When I marry it won't be on the rebound. I could get married whenever I wanted but I'm going to make sure it's the right one. [They choose the flowers. The market people drift back to their respective stalls. SYLVIA still talks with MR BUTCHER.] When Mr Right comes along, I'll know all right. We'll have the same opinions about everything. My man will be a man; he'll have to be.

I'll have four bridesmaids, and two matrons of honour. The organ will play and it will be a spring day – before the 6th of April. We'll have a nice semi-detached house and two children.

MR BUTCHER: Hope you'll be as happy as I hope Penny will be.

[*He returns to his work and she to her stall.*]

JASON: There's a wonderful feeling in the air today. BIRTHS – MARRIAGES – DEATHS – The only things worth living for. Sonia, we must marry at once.

SONIA: Go away, you smell like a church.

JASON: I'll get you in the end.

SONIA: I don't doubt that. Only trouble, mister, is that I shall be in a box and no good to anyone six feet under.

[MR BUTCHER *whispers into* JASON'S *ear*.]

JASON: Ladies and gentlemen, may I act as master of ceremonies? Our dear friend's daughter has been married. Let's put all the stalls together and make a good spread. Come on, rouse youselves.

MR BUTCHER: Let's get together, folks, let's have a party.

MRS FISH: Oh – all right.

MRS GREEN [*agreeing but grudgingly*]: Silly waste of time.

JASON: Come on you miserable, greedy, money grabbers.

SONIA: He's talking to himself again.

JASON: Wake up, make it lively. This is a wedding. Bring out the bunting, make merry, look alive, if you can.

SONIA: I'll lend some white cloth to cover the stalls. White for purity, wasted on the younger generation. When I was a girl everyone was pure, today virgins are as rare as unicorns – still, I'll give white cloths to keep up appearances.

SYLVIA: And I'll lend flowers to decorate.

JASON: Come on, ladies, look alive, you're not dead yet – worse luck.

[*The men think this an ideal opportunity to play cards.*]

MRS GREEN: Look at them, we slave away and they play rummy. [*To husband*] Haven't you got anything better to do?

MRS FISH [*to* MR FISH]: Please have some consideration for me, for a change.

MRS BUTCHER [*to* MR BUTCHER]: Just you wait till I get you inside.

MR GREEN: The broken record's on again.

MR FISH: For Pete's sake, leave me in peace.

MR GREEN: It's a celebration, a day of joy.

MRS GREEN: Should be a day of mourning.

MRS FISH: The day I got married was the worst day of my life.

MRS GREEN: The day I got married all the flags flew at half mast.

SONIA: All the days that I got married all the whistles blew.

JASON: Come on, ladies, let's get cracking, as the woodworm said in the mahogany coffin.

[JASON *and* SONIA *organize the women. The stalls are covered with white cloths, then fruit and drink.*]

MR BUTCHER: That's me down the drain. It ain't my lucky day.

MR GREEN: Unlucky in cards, lucky in love.

MR BUTCHER: Do you know, I like women.

MR GREEN: ⎱
MR FISH: ⎰ What?

MR BUTCHER: I certainly do – but not my wife.

[*The men continue playing.* SONIA *and* JASON *stand to one side as the women get the tables ready.*]

WOMEN [*singing as they work*]:
    Money is time and time is money.
    Might as well die if you haven't any.
    Money makes the world go round.
    Oh praise thee, sweet almighty pound.
    Money is time and time is money.
    If you are broke it isn't funny,
    And our love will not grow old,
    Provided it is set in gold.
    Money is time and time is money.
    If you're rich the world is sunny,
    For money opens every door.
    Give us more and more and more and more and more –
[*Their voices trail off.*]

JASON [*pulling* SONIA *close*]: Now we are alone at last.

SONIA: Please, I'm not in the mood to be made love to. Besides, I'm a sick woman, I've got kidney trouble and neuralgia, lumbago and backache, sciatica, chilblains, a carbuncle, and a boil; plus a slight attack of mice in the attic, a plague of pigeons on the roof, and guitars in the ears. Apart from that I'm all right. Who wants you when you're old? Who cares?

JASON: I want you, and Sonia, I have a confession to make – you love me.

SONIA: You should live so long.

JASON: Darling, for days I've been in a daze. Marry me and we'll combine our businesses and play monopoly all day and night. I love you.

SONIA: You liar, you're after the money I might have saved.

JASON: I wasn't even thinking of your lousy five thousand three hundred and fifty-eight pounds. Oh, Sonia, be a sport and marry me. I love you so much I could murder you.

SONIA: If you do I won't talk to you no more. No, my heart is with my money.

JASON: Where?

SONIA: In the safe and the safe is in a safe place.

JASON: You see, Sonia, we should amalgamate. The more businesses I own the better. One helps the other out.

SONIA [*fluttering her eyelashes*]: What do you mean, Jason? I'm only an ignorant girl.

JASON: Please don't come too close. You take my breath away and you know how much I love talking. I will explain. All my trades are interrelated. As an undertaker I make room in the world for more children – more children means more marriages – more marriages means more children – more children means more insurance policies, more furniture on the never-never, more people dying of worry.

SONIA: Oh Jason, what a clever man you are.

JASON [*pinching her*]: Lend me a broom and I'll sweep you off your feet. [*Sings.*]

Let Jason help you getting wed.
He sell you a double bed,
The pills to make your mattress sing,
A hearse, a horse, anything.
Sonia, you must marry me.

SONIA: I don't believe in marriage; not even for mothers and fathers. I have always wanted to be the other woman.

JASON: When they die I pass the dresses to you – when they buy dresses, you sell them thick clothes in summer and thin clothes in winter – everyone will be dead in no time. We'll make a fortune. Excuse me, my love, but I forgot to put out my special sign. [*He goes into the shop and comes back with long canvas sign which he fixes to the front of the shop.*] It cost me a fortune – [*Reads sign:*] Jason's contemporary parlour of rest. Sleep in well-designed peace. Visit your loved ones at cut rate. Excursion coaches leave here for Highgate Cemetery every Sunday. (PS. Watches and old gold bought.)

SONIA: You'd sell your own mother.

JASON: I'm just a poor orphan. My mother was too stingy to have me. Sonia, I'm all yours.

SONIA: You bore me, darling.

JASON [*he tries to embrace her*]: Sonia! You're driving me mad.

SONIA: There ain't no such thing as a happy marriage. Sure, lots that pretend to be happy – impressing others as unhappy themselves.

JASON: Sonia, you're melting my bones. [*He tries to squeeze her.*]

SONIA [*shakes him off and wags a finger at him*]: Now don't get fresh.

JASON: How should I know what I'm doing. Marry me and I'll even find you a wife for Peter.

SONIA: You'd really do that for me? You must really be infatuous with me. I don't believe you. You'd never find a girl for my boy.

JASON: Of course I would. I swear upon my trade union card. [*Takes several papers out of pocket.*]

SONIA: No one is good enough for my sonny boy.

JASON [*ardently*]: Sonia, my darling, on my knees I beg. Marry me.

[*Gets on his knees after he has brushed the dust away.*]

SONIA [*ignoring him*]: Guess how many times I've been married?
[*He shrugs and gets up.*]

JASON: Twice? [*She shakes her head and he holds three fingers up; she shakes her head and he gulps and holds four fingers up.*] Not – four – times????

SONIA [*nodding dreamily*]: How clever of you to guess right.

JASON: It makes no difference – I still want you.

SONIA [*dreams away*]: Most of my husbands came and went in the Russian Revolution. Some great friends of mine take the salute in Red Square these days. I won't mention any names. But when they smile and wave they are really saying 'Where are you Sonia? Remember the fun we had together? Come back to Russia.'

JASON: Now I know where her son gets it all from.

SONIA: All my men were gay, handsome, and dashing, and all died young – all except Peter's father who was miserable – tired and ugly. Beautiful Dmitri was my first, he had sexy green eyes and died in Leningrad in the summer palace in the middle of winter – died of chess.

JASON: Asthma?

SONIA: No, in the middle of a game that lasted five days. The winner was my second husband – Boris – the black-hearted scoundrel of the back streets of Moscow – that's where he died of German measles in the French Hospital. I found out later he was having an affair with a Lithuanian nun. I gave her nun. His funeral was smashing. . . .

JASON: Yes? Who did it?

SONIA: You wouldn't know him.

JASON: I might.

SONIA: Max my third – died beside me in bed – we were eating marshmallow and listening to Irving Berlin – he knew how to make love. Beautiful Max with the sad black eyes. Peter's father was my fourth and here I am – never saw Russia from that day to this.

JASON: Marry me and I'll take you back.

SONIA: They don't like undertakers in Russia. Come to think of it they don't like them anywhere. I love Russia.

JASON: Why did you leave?

SONIA: To get away from my memories.

JASON: Did you?

SONIA: No. [*Sings, to Stephen Foster's 'Beautiful Dreamer'.*]
    Beautiful Russia, Queen of the earth,
    Land of my memories and place of my birth,
    Beautiful Russia, Queen of the sea,
    At night I hear you calling for me.
  Ain't that funny – people are the same all over the world – except
  from Warsaw – never trust anyone who comes from Warsaw.

JASON [*indignant*]: Why not?

SONIA: I have a feeling about it, that's all.

JASON: But I come from Warsaw – !

SONIA: Never trust yourself then.

[*During the last scene it has been getting slowly darker and now everyone in the market looks up at the sky.*]

JASON: Even the days are too stingy to last long, these days.

[*A flash of lightning followed by a crash of thunder.*]

MR BUTCHER: It's going to pour. Listen everyone, come and shelter
  in my shop and we'll all have a nice drink till my daughter gets here
  with her new husband. They're all welcome, aren't they, dear?

MRS BUTCHER: Well, we may as well kill two birds with one stone,
  seeing there's no customers about.

[*Some more lightning and thunder make them all react nervously and they quickly go into the Butcher's. There the men play cards and the women natter. JASON keeps on following SONIA around, in and out of the crowd. There is subdued merriment inside the shop but the storm continues.*]

MRS FISH: Come on, Mrs B., show us their bedroom – I bet it's
  pretty.

MR FISH: That's an idea – show us the bed – I bet it's springy.

MR GREEN: Make them an apple-pie bed. Let's sew up his pyjamas.

MRS GREEN: Don't be dirty.

MR BUTCHER: Why not? You're only young once – let's all have a
  giggle.

MRS BUTCHER: Follow me – It's all pink and beautiful – and an interior sprung blissful mattress.

[*Dirty laughter from the men as they follow* MR *and* MRS BUTCHER *upstairs. When they are no longer seen,* PETER *and* ALEX *enter.*]

ALEX: But don't you see, if she's only saving the money for you, why not take it now? We could do with that extra capital.

PETER: But that would be stealing, wouldn't it?

ALEX: Not at all, the money's yours, besides you're taking it for a good cause, aren't you? With that behind you you'll make a million.

PETER: Yep, you're right.

ALEX: What good is money in a safe? It's got to be circulating to do some good. Let's get it, then.

PETER: I'm ready.

ALEX: Just one little word of advice, because I want my conscience to be clear.

PETER: What is it?

ALEX: No matter how high you jump you always return to earth. Never lose sight of it, or you might come down with a bump. Is that quite clear?

PETER: Clear as mud. Come on, look! The safe's up there, on that ledge.

[PETER *and* ALEX *stand by Sonia's shop and* PETER *points to the safe.*]

ALEX: Grab it quickly and let's get away from here.

PETER: Inside that safe, packets and packets of lovely, filthy lucre. [*He climbs on to a chair and fiddles with the safe.*] Two – to – the left – ah – one to the right – four to the – left and it's – OPEN! [*He pulls hard at the safe door.*]

ALEX: No time for dreaming. Quick.

[PETER *pulls harder and the safe falls on his head. He tries to retain his balance but cannot and falls backward off the chair and on to the floor. Spectacular sparks and stars seem to ignite around him and in the sky.* ALEX *slaps* PETER'S *face.*]

ALEX: Wake up, wake up. You all right?

[PETER *stands up slowly. In a daze he opens the safe and takes the money, and, as he does so, the light returns; but although full on it is different from before. The shadows cast seem more unreal, the sky behind looks more intense and vivid.*]

PETER: I've got what I want. My dream's come true.

ALEX: Dreams or no dreams, let's get going.

PETER: Nothing can stop me now.

[*He turns and shakes his head and activity begins once again inside the Butcher's shop; the people come down and are dressed differently; their clothes and characteristics are slightly more stylized and emphasized. The women look like busy owls shaking their heads, disapproving of their husbands who are all lounging about smoking and drinking and playing cards.* SONIA *is fussing around and giving everyone a word, like a queen at a garden party, and* JASON *is trying to keep up with her, visually proclaiming love at every opportunity. He is dressed more sinisterly.* SYLVIA *is looking at her flowers.*

PETER *and* ALEX *are about to exit.*]

JASON [*coming out of shop*]: Ladies and gentlemen – here they come –

SONIA [*rushes out*]: Here comes the bride – dadadedum – dadadedum –

[PENNY *and* TOM *enter, she in bridal gown and he in dress suit. She is sad and he is happy. The people come out and dance around them and throw confetti – they seem gay but don't make much noise.*]

MR FISH: Isn't she pretty? Isn't she nice?

MR GREEN: Pelt them with confetti, rose petals, and rice.

MR BUTCHER: Penny darling, my joy's complete.

MRS FISH:
MRS GREEN: } She'll learn soon enough that life's not so sweet.

MRS BUTCHER: Well, come on, everyone, let's go back inside.

ALL: Isn't it lovely to see a bride?

MRS BUTCHER: Penny, you look beautiful. Thank God it's Tom and not Peter. I'm so happy for you I could cry.

PENNY: And I'm so unhappy for myself I could scream – throw confetti over me, I don't want to see him.

[*They pelt the couple with confetti and dance around the stage in single file and go back into the shop;* PENNY *sadly tags on at the end of the line.*]

PENNY [*at the door*]: You coming, Peter?

PETER: No, I'm going. [*She sadly follows the others into the shop.*]

PENNY [*to* TOM]: Would you mind if I go upstairs? I've got a terrible headache.

TOM: Not at all, darling – you stay up there, that's a good place to be. I'll come up presently.

PENNY: Thank you, Tom, you're so sweet. I don't want to see him. [*She goes upstairs.*]

[SONIA *comes to the door and* SYLVIA *looks out of the window.*]

SONIA: Peter, Peter, come inside; it's getting windy and you'll get a cold.

PENNY [*upstairs on the fire-escape or leaning out of window*]: Peter, Peter, I love you still and I always will.

SYLVIA: Peter! Pull yourself together and I'll give you another chance. Maybe.

PENNY: I love you; take me away with you.

SYLVIA: If you loved me, you'd settle down.

SONIA: If you love me there's chicken for supper.

PETER: Three women in my life but the one I want doesn't want me. Who cares? That's the way it goes. I'm off. I'm going up in the world before the world goes up before me.

SONIA: And tomorrow, Peter, if you're a good boy, I'll boil you some salmon and garnish it with cucumber.

PETER: Girls! Supergirls! Petersupermann is coming your way –

SONIA: Or maybe some halibut and white lemon sauce followed by peaches and cream.

PETER: Your dream's coming true – and I don't care what colour you are, red – yellow – white – blue or green – my Superstore is open for you – whether you are father inferior or mother superior Peter's Superstore stocks everything for everyone. I don't care what you wear and where you wear it – I don't care what you do and where you do it. Boom. Boom. I'm coming your way – watch out

38

for me in the sky. Zoom – zoom – Peter supermann – supermanic – supersonic – boom – boom – superboom – super – super –

SONIA: Come home and have a nice plate of soup.

PENNY: Peter, I'll wait for you anytime, anywhere.

SONIA: Perhaps turkey and tongue and mushroom sauce and lobster on Wednesday –

ALEX: You've got the money, you've had your say, now let's get going.

SONIA [*comes out*]: Peter, come in, there's a good boy.

PETER: I'm finished listening to you. I'm leaving for the good of myself and for the good of you and I'll return rich – You'll see.

SONIA: Peter, what have you got in your hand?

PETER: This is it, I've taken the money – good-bye Mum. A loan – you – understand – ?

SONIA: Money? Peter, don't joke about money –
    [*All the people come out of the Butcher's shop, stand around, and shake their heads.*]

SONIA: Peter, what have you done? [*She rushes into shop.*]
    [PENNY *comes down to door.*]

ALEX: Peter, let's get gone.

SONIA: Darling, the safe's open – tell me you're only joking.

PETER [*his arm around her*]: I've taken it for the best – you'll see – I'm doing this for you – for all of us.

SONIA: I think I'm going to die. Put it back, sonny boy.

PETER: You'll see, I'll make you proud of me. Good-bye.

SONIA: Go away. No, come here – How could you do this to me?

PETER: Don't cry.

SONIA: All my life I slaved and what have I got? Look! See? He's going – walking out on me. Now I've got nothing except memories, but what use are they in your old age? Who wants a destitute widow with four photos on the mantelpiece? Who'll miss me? Does he care? Go on – Go! Go! Think I care? Everything is gone – Hope you enjoy yourself – I don't think – you've stolen everything – all the money I was saving for a rainy day.

39

PETER [*sings*]: There's a woman down the road, thought she'd last
forever,

So she saved ten thousand pounds for the rainy weather.

But now she's dead, yes, now she's dead,

The worms are chewing through her head,

In the rainy – wea–ther.

[*She weeps.*] Good-bye, Mother. Thanks. I'll be seeing you.

SONIA [*she suddenly stops crying as* PETER *moves to one side with* ALEX]:
Good riddance. Ain't it strange how troubles come these days,
piling up on each other, more and more. Everything comes these
days and nothing goes – 'cept him – Go – Go – It makes my eyes
sore to look at you.

PETER: Come on, Alex, I'm ready now.

ALEX: Don't be upset – women are emotional things – she'll get over
it. We all do.

SONIA: It'll do him no good. He started off on the wrong foot.

May he lose more blood than sea in the ocean –

May he get run over and smashed –

May the ground open up and swallow him –

May the sky fall on him –

[*After her outburst, pathetically and quietly*]

Peter, please take care of yourself, don't catch cold.

[SONIA, *weeping, runs into the shop. The people go back into the
Butcher's.*

PETER *sadly plucks a flower from the flower stall and he and* ALEX
move and pass the Butcher's; PENNY *still stands by the door.*]

PENNY: Take me with you, please take me with you. I can't face it
here without you.

PETER: All right, come along. You asked for it.

[*He pulls her out of the window and carries her off across his shoulder.*
ALEX *follows him off quickly. The stage darkens and in the Butcher's
shop we see them dancing.*]

SONIA [*comes out of the shop*]: He was only kidding, he won't go far.
[*She calls him.*] Peeet–ter – Peeeter – Where are you, darling?
Supper's ready. It got dark suddenly. As you get older days don't

last so long. Tuesdays and Thursdays become one and soon they all roll in together. Then just dark and light, dark and light, until – only dark, I suppose. Still, I mustn't grumble, I must count my blessings.

[TOM, *who has been upstairs, comes out of the shop and looks around.*]

SONIA: He won't go far, will he?

TOM: No, have you seen my bride?

SONIA [*shaking her head slowly as if she realizes something*]: Come here, sonny boy, I want to tell you a few things about life.

[*He approaches and sits down beside her. He leans against her and she strokes his hair. The fading light goes out.*]

CURTAIN

ACT TWO

The dream continues but it appears that twelve years have passed. The stalls are empty and look menacing, and grotesque shadows are thrown. The shops are no longer used for selling and are all boarded up except the gown shop and Jason's funeral parlour. Before each shop is a separate little trench and before the trench a mound of earth – each mound has a crude wooden board stuck in it – reading 'FISH', 'BUTCHER', and 'GREEN'. Hooters are heard and dogs are howling. Moonlight, and in Jason's shop three figures are seen. They are indistinct and are gazing through the window. One of the figures is very small and has a tall man on each side. Their cigarettes glow in the dark.

[PETER enters, followed by PENNY and ALEX. He is now thirty and has an untidy beard. He wears the clothes of a weary traveller, clothes that are utilitarian but worn out. ALEX looks more like a tramp than ever, and PENNY looks seductive in a crude way. They are all weary but furtive, looking over their shoulders as they enter. ALEX carries the few bundles. They are all obviously feeling cold.]

PETER: This is it. This is where we stay tonight.

ALEX: Don't like the look of it.

PETER: I'm not asking you. [He points to his old stall.] We'll make ourselves comfortable here. Seems safe enough.

[ALEX shrugs and puts the things down. PENNY starts preparing some food for them while ALEX unpacks. PETER sits down and smokes. The two tall men come out of the shop, but are not seen by the trio. They are about to pounce on them, but the little man pulls them back. We briefly see that the little man is JASON.]

PENNY: Doesn't he know where we are?

ALEX: Doesn't seem to. It's changed so much it had me fooled.

PENNY: Shall I tell him?

ALEX: Not yet. Can't stand another blow up. Peace at any price, that's my motto from now on.

PENNY: So that's my home then – my old safe womb – [*She shrugs and carries on with the food.*]

[*We now hear a high shrill sound, far away and dreamlike. We don't at first realize that it is* JASON *in the shop calling Peter's name.*]

JASON: PEEEET – TERR – PEEET – TERR – PEET – TERR –

[*He carries on like this.* PETER *suddenly jumps up.*]

PETER: Who's that? Did you hear that?

ALEX: It was just a dog howling.

PETER: No. Someone's calling me.

PENNY: There are plenty of mad dogs about.

JASON: PEET – TERR.

PETER: I told you. Now will you believe me?

PENNY: It's your imagination; it's just kids playing.

[PETER *walks around but does not see his mother's shop. He sits down for a moment and wipes his hands over his eyes like a confused man.*]

ALEX [*sitting down*]: Oh my poor plates of meat! Got a corn plaster, darling?

[PENNY *searches in her bag and gives him one.*]

[*Takes off shoes and socks and puts plaster on.*] What a relief! I've got one foot in the grave, and the other's got ingrowing toenails.

[*They both laugh.*]

PETER [*rushes over*]: What's going on here? What have you got to laugh at?

ALEX: Nothing and everything.

PETER: Well, stop it then. I don't feel like laughing. You got me into this bloody mess and now you expect me to get us out of it. [*To* ALEX] A fine bloody guide you turned out to be. Uranium! You lousy liar – it was always the next country where we would strike it rich – the next field was greener – Well, I was the green one all right – Stole all my mother's money and it all led nowhere. And now I'm a no one with nothing. This is where we break up. This is the end of the road.

ALEX: You said it, this *is* the end of the road. This is where I came in.

PETER: What do you mean?

ALEX: This is your home?

PETER: *Home.*

ALEX: Sweet Home.

[PETER *sweeps all the things off his old stall and then rushes to his mother's door.*]

PETER: Mother! Open up! Let me in, I'm home. [*He bangs on the door.*] [*When he realizes that there is no response he bangs on all the doors but avoids Jason's where the men duck out of sight.*]

Hey there! Where's everyone? Listen everybody – I'm home! [*He bangs and rattles on all the doors again until he is back at his mother's door.* ALEX *looks on, but* PENNY *stretches herself along the stall and lies down.*]

Mum! Where are you? This is me! Wake up! Peter Mann's come home.

ALEX [*to* PENNY]: No wonder everyone's run away.

PETER [*returning to* ALEX]: Don't understand it and I don't like it. [*To* PENNY] What are you doing lying down?

PENNY: This is the position you got me used to.

PETER: The position you begged for. [*Once more he returns to his mother's shop.*] Open up! Let me in! [*When he sees it is quite hopeless he quietly sits down outside.*] A house to let, no rent to pay, knock on the door and run away. I used to play that. But where are the kids now? They've all gone. I'm all alone. [*He closes his eyes.*]

PENNY [*gets up and goes to him*]: Please, Peter, pull yourself together.

PETER: Leave me alone.

ALEX: Pull up your socks, son.

PETER: I might if I had some. [*He reveals the fact that he has no socks; they both laugh.*] What have I got to laugh at? I'm fed up with supporting you.

ALEX: That's rich – I did all the supporting, I did all the odd jobs.

PETER: Liar.

PENNY: Shut up the pair of you. Lying on my back I supported the both of you.

PETER: Get out of my sight – Get lost.

THE DREAM OF PETER MANN

ALEX [*starts to walk away*]: All right, if that's the way you want it –

PETER: Hey, come back – where are you going?

ALEX: You just told me to –

PETER: Trust you to walk out on me when the going gets a bit tough.

ALEX: Oh – I wish you'd make up your mind. [*He wanders near Jason's shop, tests the walls, and sings:*] Oh, the walls are thin in London town – they wouldn't need much blowing down, so workers of the world unite, before we vanish in the night – my dreams are thin and wearing thinner, no one expects me home for dinner, oh, comrades of the universe, there's nothing better but plenty worse. [*He sits down.*] Think I'll have a game of chess. [*Takes pocket chess out and starts playing.*] Oh dear, what a life – now let's see, my right hand won last time – stop talking to yourself, Alex, stop talking, you'll spoil the game – I must have silence when I play – Oh all right – shut up – Thank you.

PETER [*sitting outside mother's shop and* PENNY *lying on the stall for a moment are composed in their separate worlds*]: No one! Can't trust anyone – look at him – look at her – What can you do? What can you do with them?

[JASON *creeps out behind* ALEX. *Quietly he beckons* JOHN *and* JACK *who grab* ALEX *quickly and quietly; they carry him struggling into the shop.*]

[*Looking up just after they have all gone into shop.*] What did I tell you? Run out on me – you'll be the next –

PENNY: Never. I'll never leave you.

PETER: Go, who cares? [*Gets up.*] Alex? Where are you? Come back – I didn't mean it –

[PENNY *gets up and goes to him.*]

PENNY: Don't be afraid, I'm with you.

PETER: Afraid? I'm afraid of no one – go on – get cracking, you whore – there's your own street door – [*He knocks on Mrs Green's door.*] Sylvia, where are you? I'm home.

PENNY: Grow up – For years I've been hearing about stinking Sylvia – why didn't you carry her off?

PETER: Sylvia! Let me in!

PENNY: Listen, Peter, I love you for what you are – I'm real – I'm not a vision –

PETER: You said it – You're a tart, a trollop, you make me sick.

PENNY: I'm what you made me, but I don't hold that against you. Don't you see, you're all washed up, but I don't care because I am also –

PETER: What can I do? Penny, where can I go?

PENNY: We'll start again here – Business as usual.

PETER: Not here. Never crap on your own doorstep. [*He turns away from her and goes back to his mother's shop.* PENNY *sadly returns to her mother's door.*] We haven't been gone long – go home – they'll forgive you.

PENNY: Maybe, but I'll never forgive myself.

[JASON'*s men grab her and take her inside.*]

PETER: Penny, come here – where are you? Mum, let me in – Sylvia! Alex, where are you? Penny, don't leave me!

[JASON *comes out.* PETER *sees him across the stage but does not recognize him at first. They stealthily creep towards each other.* JASON *is dressed in frock coat and top hat and carries a baton under his arm.*]

Stop! Don't come closer.

JASON [*taking out a cosh, holds it in striking position, then offers it to the young man*]: It's dangerous to be out alone these days – can I interest you in a cosh, or a knuckle-duster? Haven't I seen you before, somewhere? On Tele maybe or in the rogues' gallery.

PETER: Jason, it's me.

JASON [*shines a torch in his face*]: Strike a light, look who it ain't. So the salmon has come back to be tinned, definitely grade three.

PETER: I've been through a hard time.

JASON: Can I interest you in some life insurance or a ticket to the policeman's ball?

PETER: Stop joking – Where's everyone?

JASON: Indoors, afraid and shivering under bedclothes.

PETER: Why? Afraid of whom?

JASON: Of strangers – like you.

PETER: *Me?* I'm not a stranger.

JASON [*takes out a mirror*]: Take a look at yourself – Would you trust that man? Never! Can I sell you a razor?

PETER: But it's me, Peter Mann –

JASON: Try and tell them that. Now look, I like you and want to help, but I know you won't be welcome here.

PETER: But this is my home!

JASON: It was, but *twelve years* is a long time.

PETER: Twelve years? But I only left – a few months ago.

JASON: That's the way time flies.

PETER: But it seems like yesterday. What can I do?

JASON: Sorry, if your face don't fit you're out in the cold. Good-bye.

PETER: I want my mother. She'll vouch for me. [*Bangs on door.*] Mum! Where are you? [*To* JASON] Where can I go?

JASON: That's your headache. Now – be a good boy and go. The people won't come out until you've gone. And they've got to work in order to get the food to make them work. Ta ta.

PETER: I won't go. You can't scare me. I know my rights. I'll call the police.

JASON: At your service – I am the police – why do you think I wear this hat? Here's my badge. Now do I have to blow my whistle for my two legged bow-wows?

PETER: But what happened? What are these holes for? Everything's changed? Why?

JASON: Twelve years ago you had an idea and went to look for it – URANIUM! The fever spread here and everywhere. They stopped making love, stopped buying and selling, neglected the business, and everything went to rack and ruin. To cut a long story sideways, everybody started digging, each his own little pitch. People were like animals and the governments ran away – everywhere the same story. Westminster barricaded itself from Marylebone, streets cut themselves off from each other – everyone cringing in his little corner. Nobody wanders out and nobody wanders in – or – [*Makes a throat-cutting sign with his hand across his throat.*] Twelve years, and we're still digging, and found nothing but worms, bones, and nails, and we're tired but who knows? Something may turn up. The most intelligent person in each district usually takes charge of things – that's me – [*He blows his whistle and the men come on.*] who usually hires tough guys, that's them – [*Indicates the two men who by now are close to* PETER.] to get rid of scroungers and strangers – that's you. Good day.

    [PETER *makes one last desperate attempt to break into his mother's shop and get away from men – he is about to throw his weight against it when she opens the door and he falls inside.*]

SONIA: They fall at my feet these days. [JASON *waves his men away.*] What can I do for you, sonny boy?

PETER [*picking himself up*]: Mother! I'm home. [*He tries to kiss her.*]

SONIA: I may be an attractive woman, but I draw the line at cradle snatching.

PETER: Mother – I'm home – it's me – Peter. Please forgive me.

SONIA: I forgive you, but who are you? Peter? Peter? Let me see?

PETER: Mother – they're after me – don't let them get me.

SONIA: Who? [*She looks around and* JASON *puts his finger to his temple denoting Peter's madness;* SONIA *nods.*]

PETER: Help me, please; I'm hungry, cold, and tired.

SONIA: You're a nice-looking kid but I can't help you.

PETER: But I'm Peter – your son.

SONIA: I have no son.

PETER: It must be my beard – you don't know me because of this.

SONIA: If I had a son do you think I would let him grow a beard – sorry, son.

PETER [*with horror walks away*]: Penny, where are you? Alex – Let's get away from here. [*He searches for them.*]

JASON: So you don't know him?

SONIA [*to* JASON]: When you've got money everybody's related to you. When you've got nothing you've got no one.

JASON: We'll have to make an example of him – he's an impostor.

SONIA: Pity – such a nice kid, too – still, we can't take any chances these days, besides look at his face – it's all jaw and no forehead.

[*All the people come out and start digging in the trenches. They look tired and take no notice of each other or of* PETER. *They are furtive and wear rags.*]

PETER: Alex! Quick! Come back – let's get away from here!

[JASON *blows a whistle;* JOHN *and* JACK *appear, and all the people stop working.* PETER *backs away from them and falls in a trench. They grab him and pinion him, and the market people applaud.*] Let me go – let me go.

[*They tie Peter to a stall.*]

JASON: Bring the others!

[JOHN *and* JACK *go off and bring back* ALEX *and* PENNY *who are tied up – one on each side of* PETER.]

PETER: Oh, there you are – at last. If it hadn't been for you I wouldn't be here.

ALEX: Who led us here in the first place?

PENNY: Stop arguing, you two – we're all in the same boat.

[*The market people gather around and now seem quite happy with the proceedings.*]

JASON: Well, friends – let's have some hush please. As you can see we have strangers. What shall we do with them?

MR BUTCHER: Maybe they know some new card games.

MRS BUTCHER: Don't trust them.

MRS FISH: They might steal from us.

MR FISH: They'd find it hard.

MRS GREEN: What do they want?

MR GREEN [*to* PETER]: If you want my old woman – it's a deal.

MRS FISH: They might be spies from Bow, or murderers from Soho.

MRS BUTCHER: Or thieves from Shepherd's Bush after the gold fillings in my teeth.

MRS GREEN: Or white slavers after virgins.

MR GREEN: They'd go bankrupt round here.

JASON: Silence! I don't care who they are or why they've come – All I know is they are up to no good –

SONIA: Oh, smack their bums and send them packing.

JASON: No! I am the law here! And I don't know about you but I'm tired of spies and foreigners – we must show the world who we are.

JOHN: Hear –

JACK: Hear!

PETER: I've been too stunned to speak, lost for words to see how my old friends have changed, but now I'm appealing to you – Please – look – look at my face – I'm Peter Mann – shave off my beard, honestly – I swear I am – on the Bible!

JASON: Bible? [*He shrugs.*] Don't use that dirty word – you make the ladies blush. *We* don't have books any more. Haven't you heard?

PETER: Look, you know who I am.

PENNY: It's no good, Peter; they don't want to recognize us.

PETER: Sylvia! She's the one. Yes. Sylvia! Sylvia! Where are you?

JASON: Bung up his gullet, boys, he's splitting my ear drum.

PETER: I promise not to scream.

[JASON *waves his men away.* SYLVIA *comes out of Green's house. She looks much fatter now and is getting grotesque to look at.*]

SYLVIA: Did someone call me? [*She goes up to* PETER.] What is this? [*She sniffs and shudders.*] They pong.

PETER: Oh go away. Sylvia – where are you?

SYLVIA: I'm Sylvia – who are you?

PETER: Peter. But you're not Sylvia. SYLVIA! SYLVIA!

JASON: I warned you.

SYLVIA: Peter? I don't know you.

PETER: If you are Sylvia, tell them to let me go, for old time's sake. Remember the times we had together – I was the first to touch you – you said so.

SYLVIA: The bloody nerve – how dare you. I'm a respectable girl – I'd never mix with the likes of you.

PETER: Oh go away – go away – I can't bear to look at you. Gag me, blindfold me, I don't care any more.

ALEX [*calls* JASON *over*]: Get it over quickly, he's a sensitive lad. [JASON *nods.*] And please untie me, I won't run away. Anything will seem like a picnic after travelling around with him.

JASON: You have my sympathies. [*He unties* ALEX *who starts to play chess again.*] Dear friends – quiet please. I demand that we set an example with this liar.

JOHN: You said it.

JACK: You certainly did.

JASON: For your good. For the good of the community I demand the full works.

JOHN: Hear –

JACK: Hear!

JASON: He must die –

PETER: Hey – a joke's a joke –

[JOHN *puts his hand over Peter's mouth.*]

JASON: Then the outside world will know that we don't like strangers in the market-place.

MRS BUTCHER: Quite right!

MRS FISH: Serves him right.

MRS GREEN: We've got to be careful.

SONIA: Count me out – you're all doing your nut.

JASON: We'll let the others go – both of them – [*indicating* ALEX *and* PENNY.] After they've seen what we've done to him they will tell the world.

ALEX: King out of danger.

PENNY: I won't go without him – if you kill him you can kill me too.

JASON: Silly girl. Why are you dying to die? You'll do as you're told.

[JACK *releases* PENNY *and she goes to* ALEX *who continues to play chess.*]

PENNY: How can you play at a time like this?

ALEX: He's got out of worse scrapes.

PENNY: No, this time it's serious.

ALEX: He'd talk his way out of hell.

PENNY: They'll kill him. Alex, we must do something.

ALEX: Don't worry. Call me when he goes green around the gills – I'll believe it then.

[PENNY *rushes to* PETER.]

JOHN: Three cheers –

JACK: For Jason – Hip – Hip – Hip –

SONIA: *Horrors!* You give me the horrors.

JOHN AND JACK: For he's a jolly good fellow – for he's a jolly good fellow –

JASON: For I'm a jolly good fellow –

SONIA: That's something I can deny.

JASON: *Sonia!* Aren't you proud of me? Everyone is safe again, thanks to me. Marry me tomorrow and we will merge in every way.

SONIA: Not on your life – business and pleasure don't mix.

JASON [*to* PETER]: Well, how do you want to go out? [*To* JOHN] Take the gag off and let him have a few last words.

PETER: Mum, save me. Penny, help me.

PENNY: If only I could.

JASON: Have you a last wish?

PETER: Yes. I don't want to die.

[*The gag is replaced.*]

JASON: You're mad, death is very fashionable these days – the very best people are dying like flies.

ALEX: Please be quieter. My knight is in a sticky position.

MRS BUTCHER: Come on, Jason, let's get cracking.

MR BUTCHER: If you must do it – quick and clean – through the forehead with a bullet.

MRS FISH: Put a sock in it. We haven't seen a good show for years.

MR FISH: Bash him on the head, then – that's the best way – and slit his gullet.

MR GREEN: Chop him up, peel him, boil him, bake him, mash him – do what you like but get it over with – the poor boy's had enough.

MRS GREEN: Trust you. You want everything quick – have it and turn to the wall – well, women are different.

MRS BUTCHER: I love a bit of ceremony.

MRS FISH: It's not often we can let off steam.

JASON [*to* PETER]: If you know any prayers, say them now.

SONIA: Let the poor boy speak.

[*The men are playing cards, and altogether there is a festive air around.* SYLVIA *and* JACK *bring on drinks from Jason's shop while* JOHN *guards* PENNY *and* ALEX.]

SONIA [*who is offered a drink by* SYLVIA]: No thanks.

SYLVIA: It's very nice – it's a bloody Mary – Tomato juice and vodka. [*She hands the drinks around.*]

SONIA: Take off his gag.

[JASON *does so.*]

PETER: HELLLLLLLLLP.

JASON: Save your breath, you ain't got much coming.

PETER: This is my home – where I worked – you must know me. That was my stall. Step right up, you know me – I'm the one – everyone knows me – I'm the man – Peter Mann.

JASON: Poor boy's demented.

PETER: I sold cloth here – I know all the patter. Give me a chance. Alex – tell them you found me here.

ALEX: I found him here. [*Continues with chess.*] Sssh – this is crucial.

PETER: Penny darling – tell them.

PENNY: Please believe him, this was my home, too. What's the matter with all of you? *Stop it!* Oh, Peter, what can I do? Let him go! Use me as an example. Kill me. I haven't got much to lose – only the things I don't even have. Peter, I'm staying with you.

PETER: My stall – [*Peter breaks away and jumps on stall.*] My stall – [*He stands before it between the two men.*] Step right up – Ladies and gentle–men – I've got a little line today – the finest, toughest, purest, softest, guaranteed drip-dry, heat resistant, mothproof cloth this side of the Table Mountain – you there – feel it – smell it – see that mark? Made by Mann for Man – I'm knocking them out – not fifty shillings – not forty, not thirty-five, not thirty but going to the first ten lucky punters for a measly nicker – Show us the colour of your money – That's the best colour in the world – I'm mad – I'm crazy, I'm stone bonks – I should be locked away giving such bargains. Look at these shirts – Come on, buy, you silly sods – Nylon négligées, lingering lingerie, and beautiful bras for bonny bits of –

[*The men get hold of* PETER.]

JASON: Don't worry, son, I've got a padded coffin just your size, and it's almost closing time.

PENNY [*rushes to him*]: Peter – [*The men try to drag her away.*] No, let me hold on to him –

JASON: All right, let her stay – I was in love once. I was young once.

SONIA: Don't kid me – you were born just as you are.

PETER: Penny – now I know – if I had another chance I swear I'd be different – it's you I really want.

PENNY: I know, darling. Hold on – I'm holding on to you. You're not alone.

PETER: We're all alone in the end. Penny, forgive me.

MR BUTCHER: Get a move on.

MR FISH: Look at them, love's young dream.

MR GREEN: If I had a fiddle I'd play 'Hearts and Flowers'.

MRS GREEN: Shut up – these men – lovely show, ain't it?

MRS BUTCHER: Proper smashing.

MRS FISH: Real romantic.

SYLVIA: Popcorns! Chocolate! Cigarettes! [*She wanders around.*]

ALEX: Checkmate!

JASON: All right, boys, this is it.

> [JOHN *and* JACK *stand* PETER *on the stall and tie his outstretched hands with white ribbons which they tie to either end of the stall.* PENNY *clutches his feet and buries her face into his flesh.*]

Now, something spectacular like stabbing.

> [JOHN *and* JACK *take out knives and are about to fall on him.*]

PETER: I want to say a few last words.

JOHN: You've said enough.

JACK: You said it.

JASON: All right boys – I know how you must be feeling – like turkey to roast and no shillings for the slot. A few last words and be quick about it –

PETER: God guide me –

JASON: No prayers, no philosophy – hurry up, my boys are already on time and a half.

PETER: Where was I? Oh yes – listen God – I didn't mean to steal –

54

Seriously – look here – What? I can't hear you – come closer – I'm so lonely – everyone's gone – even you –

JASON: No filibustering.

SONIA: Leave the poor devil alone – he's talking to God.

JASON: He's a liar.

SONIA: Would God talk to a liar?

PETER: Oh guide me – I'm afraid – I've got land sickness, sea sickness, and sky sickness – get me out of this and I'll make it worth your while – oh – Dad! Dad! Come home – where are you? Stop wandering – Oh God come home – the days play fast and loose with me and the noose of night strangles my prayers – please understand even if you're not there – just in case – come downstairs and pull your pyjamas up – take the cotton wool out of your ears – stop tripping over your beard – lead me out of this – lift me up – hold me – lift me up – not too far from earth – put me down not too far from the stars – Dad – come home – Oh God – Where am I? Where are you? Who am I? Who are you? What am I? Why am I? When am I?

JASON: Enough – that should put you in his good books. Carry on, boys.

SONIA [rushes to them just as the men are about to lunge their daggers in]: WAIT!

JASON: What now?

SONIA: You cannot kill him – he's my – son – that's who you are.

PETER: Mother – thank God! The nightmare's over.

SONIA: You are a silly boy – why didn't you tell me? [She climbs up beside him.]

JOHN: What now, boss?

JACK: Yes, what next?

JASON: Be patient, boys – we'll iron the whole thing out – have a fag. [They do.] Sonia – are you sure he's your boy? Why didn't you recognize him before?

SONIA: I wasn't too proud of him – wanted to forget him – but blood is thicker than water. Why didn't you tell me?

JASON: If you didn't recognize him why should I?

SONIA: You know everything. After my money still – you naughty, nasty old man. I'm surprised with you.

JASON: Are you sure you're sure?

SONIA: I heard him cry for help – a mother knows – yes under all that bum fluff he's all mine. Untie him.

JASON: I'll think it over. We won't be hasty. [*He goes and speaks softly to his two men.*]

SONIA: Please hurry up, I've got a chicken in the oven.

[PENNY *embraces* PETER *and to avoid her parents she goes to talk to* ALEX.]

MRS GREEN: What a bloody shame – looks like the show's over.

MRS BUTCHER: It's always the same. Nothing ever happens round here.

MR BUTCHER: Good luck, son – but go while the going's good.

MRS FISH: Back to work, then – come on –

[*All the wives drag all their husbands back to their respective trenches.*]

PETER: Thank you – how can you forgive me? How can I repay you? I'm free! Free again – free – I'm flying – nothing can stop me – I'm alive – [*He flaps his arms and though he is still tied with ribbons he resembles a bird.*] I'm saved – cockledoodledo. Mother – I want to kiss you.

SONIA: Mother? Look, when they untie you, you hoppit – I've got enough worries. I'm not your mother – and if I was I wouldn't want to be.

PETER: But you are. You said you were.

SONIA: I couldn't bear to see you suffer – not even you – so I took pity. I've got a heart, ain't I? But I'm a hard woman, so don't take advantage.

PETER: But you *are* my mother – you really are. I'm Peter.

SONIA: I have no son – apart from being a low life he's also touched – poor boy – Listen, I took pity on you, but when they untie you – you fly. Only I could have done it, only I can influence that **body** snatcher, so take my advice and toodle loo.

PETER: But – I am – you are –

JASON [*as his men untie* PETER]: Welcome home, Peter – I'm so pleased I bumped into you before you leave.

PETER: Leave? What do you mean?

JASON: You can't stay here – it's too small for both of us.

PETER: I won't go – you need me here.

JASON: Sonia – either he goes or I stay.

SONIA: Sort it out between you – my chicken's nearly done.

PETER: Chicken? Oh, Mum, I'm starved.

JASON: We've got enough mouths to feed without you.

SONIA [*to* PETER]: You heard what he said – Tata, sonny boy –

PETER: But –

SONIA: Look, son, I saved your life – what more do you expect? Chicken as well? In these times – ?

JASON: You heard what she said. Even your mother's had enough – Good-bye. [*He turns to* SONIA.] Sonia, at last – now I know you're free. No longer holding on to pipe dreams in the sky – and now you've got rid of your son – maybe you'll listen to reason. Marry me.

SONIA: But what's your real reason? Because I can cook? *No!* Because I'm beautiful? *No!* Because I might have a few bob saved? *Yes!*

JASON: Marry me now – I'll marry us – I'll sell myself a ring – buy some furniture and insurance from myself – and we'll keep it in the family. I love you – you're so lovely – so gay – so tender and understanding – so – my shape – I dream about you.

SONIA: You dirty old man – you make me shiver, besides you don't wash behind your ears –

JASON: You do things to me – I'm your slave. I can't live without you. Oh, Sonia, how like a woman you are –

SONIA: That's only a coincidence. Let's talk about you for a change. What do you think of me? Good-bye.

[SONIA *goes into her shop.*]

JASON: I think you're a horrible, terrible, ugly old woman – a heartless monster, with no fine feeling. [*He turns to* PETER.] Now you go quick before we string you up again. We don't want you round here.

[*The two men close on him.*]

PENNY: Come on, Peter, let's get going.

[*One man gives* ALEX *a prod.*]

ALEX: The people in the next field may be greener. Oh my poor legs – will I ever rest?

PETER [*to the people in the separate trenches*]: Listen everyone – listen to me – dreamers, schemers, slaves, slobs – Down your tools and listen –

JASON: Don't listen to him if you know what's good for you. Jack – John! Frogmarch him away.

PETER: I've got something to tell you. Something to sell you.

[JOHN *and* JACK *have grabbed him, but the people come out of their trenches.*]

MR GREEN: Leave him alone – listen to what he's got to say.

MR BUTCHER: He can't make things worse.

PETER: There needs to be a new spirit – a new feeling – a revival of hope.

MRS BUTCHER: Hope? What's that?

ALEX: Hold on to your safety belts, here we go again.

MR BUTCHER [*to* JOHN *and* JACK]: Let him go – speak up, son.

MR FISH: Where there's life there's hope.

PETER: I can give you hope.

MRS FISH: Will hope light the gas? Will it fill the belly?

MR BUTCHER: Let him go or we'll brain ya – [*the three men stand ready to hit* JOHN *and* JACK.]

JASON: All right, let him go.

PETER [*stands on a soapbox*]: Thank you one and all – Now, what are you digging for?

MR BUTCHER: Uranium!

PETER: Exactly! Then I'm the boy for you. We must organize, co-operate, work together.

MRS BUTCHER: Work together? You mad?

PETER: Why are you all digging your own grave – erm – trench – ? You there? What have you found? Nothing! Many hands make light – how does it go?

ALEX: Too many cooks spoil the broth?

PETER: Oh shut up, Judas. You must pool resources – pull together – work in harmony – share the labour, share the treasure. You must dig a supertrench – and you need me as supervisor.

ALEX: Yeah, the supermanic depressive visionary.

PENNY: Leave him alone. He's trying. You've been needling him for days.

ALEX [*to* PENNY]: Let's go.

PETER: There's nothing I don't know about uranium – ask my friends here – is that right?

ALEX: Absolutely – he doesn't know – a thing.

PETER: You want me – and I want you to want me – I promise you the earth –

ALEX: They'll get it all right.

PETER: What have you got to lose?

MRS BUTCHER: Nothing!

JOHN: Shall we do him, boss?

JACK: Give the word.

JASON: Not yet.

PETER: We'll become strong again – this place will be the centre of the world – we'll set an example to all the streets in the country – what do you say?

MR FISH: Sounds like hard work.

PETER: Sure – but who's afraid of hard work?

MEN: We are.

PETER: Nonsense – you've had no incentive – nothing to work for – but now we must dig, dig, dig – off with your coats and on with the job. Up with your hearts and down with your shovels.

[*This is met with silence.*]

What's the matter with you all?

MR BUTCHER: We're afraid.

PETER: What of?

MR FISH: This, that, and the other.

MR GREEN: Especially the other.

MRS GREEN: I'm afraid of myself.

MR BUTCHER: I'm afraid of my wife.

MRS BUTCHER: I'm afraid of my brother.

MR FISH: We're afraid of each other.

MR GREEN: I'm afraid of my mother – and she's scared to death of me.

MRS GREEN: Who could blame her? I'm afraid of my shadow.

WOMEN: We're afraid of having kids.

MEN: We're afraid of sterility –

MRS FISH: Afraid of virility.

MR BUTCHER: Afraid of frigidity.

MRS GREEN: Rigidity.

MRS FISH: Potency.

MR FISH: Impotency. Oh, we're so afraid.

PETER: I'm afraid you all worry too much.

MR BUTCHER: What's the answer?

PETER: I am. Peter Mann.

MRS GREEN: If only we could believe that.

WOMEN: We need someone to lead us.

MEN: We need someone to need us. . . .

PETER: Your worries are over, because – I'm taking over.

ALL: Hurrah – hurrah –

[*They lift him up and carry him around the stage.* SONIA *comes rushing out and so does* TOM GROOM *looking just like in Act One, only much older – his wedding clothes still on but looking rather dilapidated.* JASON *retires to the back of the stage with his men, and* ALEX *sits down and plays chess:* PENNY *tries to keep close to* PETER, *but* SYLVIA *keeps on coming in between her and the happy group.*]

PETER: Listen, everyone – and when we find uranium – we'll open the greatest – longest – highest – grandest Superstore – you ever saw – selling the most wonderful superfood in the world – lovely fresh salmon – peaches and cream – fat turkeys – hams and tongues – lobster and barons of beef – legs of pork – shoulders of veal – lettuces the size of currant bushes – cucumbers – tomatoes – dates – melons – olives – kippers – marmalade –

SONIA: Peter! You are my Peter – my son – you're back – at last you're back.

PETER [*the people put him down*]: At last you know me – Oh, Mum, I'm starving.

SONIA: Where have you been? I've looked all over for you! You bad boy – you're so pale and thin – your eyes are bloodshot – too many late nights, eh?

PETER: Days and nights have been the same. Let's go inside.

SYLVIA: Oh, Peter – darling Peter – I love you – I've been waiting for you – please don't leave me again.

PETER: Sylvia – I dreamed of this moment.

SONIA: Jason, I want you.

JASON: Sonia darling. [*He embraces her; she pushes him off.*]

SONIA [*takes off Jason's hat and puts it on* PETER]: Here is my son and he's taking over.

JASON: I'll be happy to place myself and my boys at his disposal – at a slight cost, of course. Oh, Sonia, Sonia, it seems like I've lost you again. Never mind – I'll get you in the end.

SONIA: Don't be dirty. Come, Peter, I've got a bone to pick with you – a nice roast chicken – and some lovely soup to start with – oh what can I do with you? Do me a favour, shave that beard off. Oh you drive me mad – you'll be the death of me – what a son I've got! Did you miss me, darling? What did you do with that money? Where have you been? Thief! Liar! Worm – darling – am I happy to see you!

SYLVIA: Peter, we'll get married as soon as possible.

MRS GREEN: Let's all have a party.

MRS FISH: That's a marvellous idea.

[*They all become merry.*]

PETER [*about to enter house*]: No! This is the time to work – we must dig – break down barriers – dig together – fast and deep – Now is the time – I'll see you all later.

[PETER, SONIA, *and* SYLVIA *go inside where they drink.*]

ALEX: What did I tell you? He's out of trouble and we're out in the cold. Typical! Look at him! We worry ourselves sick, and greedy-guts in there guzzles himself sick. I'm a bloody mug and you're a bloody fool.

PENNY: You're right, Alex. Let's get away from here –
   [*The people start digging again – this time more feverishly – watched by* JOHN *and* JACK. PENNY *goes close to* TOM GROOM, *watching him.*]
JASON [*to* ALEX]: Excuse me, how would you like to earn a fiver?
ALEX: How many people must I kill?
JASON: Just get rid of Peter Mann. Spin him a yarn – get him away from here – as far as possible.
ALEX: Nothing doing, I'm in the middle of my game.
JASON: Twenty pounds?
   [ALEX *shakes head.*]
   Forty? Forty-one? Fifty? Seventy-five? All right – I'll have to do it. One hundred pounds?
ALEX: Not interested. Sssh – my left hand is sensitive [*playing chess*].
JASON: You must take him away.
ALEX: And stop shouting. My right hand suffers from ear trouble. Good night.
JASON: In that case I shall go inside and enjoy the party. I'm a realist – what else could any honest undertaker afford to be? [*He knocks on the door and* PETER *opens it and inside they all dance;* ALEX *plays quietly, and* PENNY *talks to* TOM.]
TOM: Are you lost, Miss?
PENNY: Yes, I have been but I've come home. Tom!
TOM: How do you do? You know my name? Of course. I'm the fellow who's pointed at and jeered after. I have a room here [*points at Mr and Mrs Butcher*]. You've got a nice face.
PENNY: Are you still waiting?
TOM: What else is there to do?
PENNY: You must love her a lot.
TOM: I'm not sure any more – I've just got into the habit. I like you.
PENNY: You poor boy. You're so different from the others; I wish I had someone like you.
TOM: I know what you are, but I don't care. I need something so bad. Please come with me inside.
PENNY: How long will you wait for her?

TOM: For ever, I think.

PENNY: Then there's no chance for me.

TOM: Sure there is. Come and pass the time with me. I'll look after you. [*He grabs her.*] Let me kiss you.

PENNY: Leave me alone. She'll never come now. Men! For someone like me, for a slut, you'd dirty your dream.

TOM: I've waited so long. She'll understand. Believe me, you're the first I've noticed.

PENNY: Bitched by myself. That's something to tell the looking-glass. She'll never come now.

TOM: Please let me help you. Let me love you. Help me.

PENNY: Come on – I'll kill two birds with one stone – besides I don't want to see him again.

TOM [*to* MRS BUTCHER]: Can she stay with me?

MRS BUTCHER: What you do in your room is your own affair. As long as you pay for it.

[PENNY *sadly follows* TOM *into the house.*]

MR BUTCHER: I've seen that girl before, somewhere.

MRS BUTCHER: You have, have you? Get on with your work.

[*Everyone is digging when* PETER *and* SYLVIA, JASON *and* SONIA *come dancing out of the house.*]

SYLVIA: Mr Jason get for me – a long white gown – a double bed –

PETER: With a springy spring –

SYLVIA: A wedding ring, a motor car – a frigidaire –

PETER: Not so frigid –

SYLVIA: A three-piece suite –

SONIA: And lots to eat.

SYLVIA: Jason get me everything.

PETER: Put up the banns, pull down the blinds – for my darling you are mine – we'll be rich and great – the very greatest – every gadget we get will be the latest –

ALL: Jump into bed – good-bye maidenhead –

PETER: Oh tonight you will be mine –

ALL: Up with the lights – let's all get stinking tight – we're gonna have a smashing time.

[*Everyone dances around and the four dance back into the house. The people in the trench work furiously but now are all happy. Drink has appeared and they are all swigging it.*]

ALEX [*finishing the game*]: Checkmate. [*He sits down on a stall and covers himself over as the Act ends.*]

CURTAIN

ACT THREE

Five more years have passed. It is summer. At the back of the stage, where the shops once stood, there is now a modern-looking building. This is the shroud factory. The trenches are now gone, but down-stage there is a concrete slab that covers a passageway down into the earth; this has a very heavy metal door with the word 'SHELTER' in red lettering.

The undertaker's and the gown shop are still there, but look very prosperous. The shutters of Sonia's shop are up but there are no more gay-looking dresses and no more materials.

Flowers surround the door and windows and inside there is great luxury, though the furniture is a terrible mixture of contemporary and nouveau riche.

[*Inside* SONIA *lies on a divan, asleep.* SYLVIA *is with her, looking very fat, in fact very much the way Sonia did in Act One.*

SYLVIA *looks obscene with gaudy clothes and a great deal of chunky jewellery. Her hair is dyed platinum blonde and she is heavily made up.* PETER *is with them, but is looking outside, where all the stalls have been pushed away from the centre of the stage.*

On one stall languish PENNY *and* ALEX; *he is playing chess.*

The market people have lost the hunted, haunted look of the previous Act: now they are vacant and robot-like. They are all dressed in dull uniform dungarees and are seated centre-stage in a circle. TOM GROOM *addresses them. In the factory* JASON *stands between his two men.*]

TOM: Come on, once again –
MEN: We're tired.
TOM: Come on, on your feet – all together – One, two – one, two, three – We don't want a shroud factory. One, two, three, four – Where is our Superstore? Oh, what's the use? What are we on strike for if you're gonna sit down?
WOMEN: This is a sit-down strike.

TOM: That's what you think. Up you lazy bastards – [*They all groan as they slowly get up.*] One, two – three, four – We don't want war – One, two, three, four, five –

ALL: We want to stay alive. [*They all carry little posters as they walk around and around – reading*] – We demand more money – we want peace. No Union – No Work.

JASON [*suddenly rushes out followed by* JOHN *and* JACK]: Now come on, back to work, and then we can start negotiations.

TOM: We stay on strike till we get our rights.

JASON: Everything will get better, we are thinking of you all the time. And if you want a union – well, certainly, I will organize it and run it for you.

MR BUTCHER: We want a Superstore, not a superwar.

JOHN: You'll get what you're given.

JACK: Shall we do them, boss?

JASON: No – we are all sensible people and we can talk it over. Please, my children, what do you want?

TOM: We all dug together, didn't we? And we found it but what happened? Peter Mann told us that so much uranium made the world a dangerous place to be so we couldn't have our Superstore just yet and we were palmed off with promises.

MR GREEN: We haven't even got a decent place to live.

TOM: So he gave us full employment and now we work the clock round in this shroud factory and he's the richest man in the world – and we haven't got a Superstore.

JASON: But these are old arguments – And when we have enough shrouds and everyone in the world is protected I personally promise you will get your Superstore. Now back to work for everything will turn out all right. Besides, what use is food if you're dead?

MRS GREEN: It's always been promises, promises, promises.

MRS FISH: Things don't get better, they get worse.

MRS BUTCHER: Everything is dearer. And look at the state of the world.

TOM: Yes, we want protection like him. We want shelter. The world is on the brink but he'll be safe. Down there in his deep shelter.

Because he's the richest he's got the deepest place to hide. We want protection.

JASON: There will not be a war, take that from me – it's only rumours you hear. Maybe a little limited war but the shrouds will protect you. Now, please for his sake – you know how he worries about you; besides poor Sonia is dying.

TOM: So are we dying. We're being wasted. We work all the time, we're going to get blown up any minute – come on everyone –

[JASON *retires to talk to his men as they march round again.*]

MEN: We found a fortune in the ground and scooped it out.

WOMEN: And in its place we set a concrete mound –

MEN: But now it isn't safe above the ground –

WOMEN: We truly have inherited the earth.

MEN: We stay on strike – we're sick of senseless work.

ALL: No peace on earth until we rest in earth.

[*The men sit down and play cards. The women stand and gossip.* JOHN *and* JACK *watch them as* JASON *rushes into Sonia's house.*]

JASON: Peter, you must do something – get them back to work. Only you can do it.

PETER: We're all going to die.

JASON: Thank God, otherwise where would I be? Peter, do something.

PETER: I brought it to this and there's no escape.

JASON: We need more shrouds. You must stop dreaming – after all the world isn't coming to an end even if we do all get blown up. I'm an optimist.

PETER: I must take my mother down.

JASON: Do what you like, but first get them back to the bench. And don't worry. Whatever you do, I'll look after the business.

PETER: *That's* my main worry. [*He goes outside.*] Listen everyone – [*He walks into the centre of the people.*] I'm one of you. We did this together. This factory – look at it – once again we can hold up our heads with pride – we led the world and we set the example – we built this Empire – all eyes are on us – and as you know we pulled the world together, it is our shrouds that cover the world – every

67

Peter Mann shroud factory in the world got the prototype and the hope and incentive from us – I was the Mann. I had the idea. I created this new industry for you – Only by working hard can we be saved; we can be saved and we must be saved. We can negotiate but it must be by strength – the enemy must know that our goods are Empire and second to none – there will be no war, I promise – cross my heart – but only, I repeat, only if each member of the community plays his part – shrouds are essential – they are for the defence of freedom and liberty – when this crisis is over I promise you – remuneration, superannuation – abolition of taxes, free television sets, and the greatest Superstore full of food – remember what it was like? Real food – three-hour day – four-day week and beautiful homes for your happy children – this is my solemn promise – now let me see you all – all of you – go back to work and everything will be forgotten.

TOM: Three cheers for dear mister Mann. Hip, hip, hip. –

ALL: Hooray – hooray – [*They line up and troop back into the factory, followed by* JOHN *and* JACK *who watch them. There they work like automatons, fast and silent.*]

[PETER *goes back inside, to his mother.*]

PETER: Mother, wake up, there's not much time.

SONIA: Oh, I was dreaming so beautifully.

PETER: Come on down, war will break out any moment.

SONIA: I'll be dead anyway in a couple of hours. What the eye doesn't see the heart cannot grieve. Now, wheel me outside, it's nice out there – the birds don't notice the crisis.

SYLVIA [*rushing to* PETER *as he prepares to take his mother from settee to a very grand-looking invalid chair*]: Take me down with you. Peter, I believe you.

SONIA: Peter, who's she? Huh! Your wife!

SYLVIA: Shut up, you interfering old bitch.

SONIA: Who's old? Come, Peter, I've only got a short time left – You owe me at least that much.

[SYLVIA *confers with* JASON *as* PETER *pushes his mother outside.* JASON *follows them, and* SYLVIA *follows on.*]

PETER: Now you must rest and take it easy.

SONIA: Now he worries about me – now, when it's too late. All my life he drives me to this point and now he wants to prolong the agony.

PETER: In a minute we'll be down in the shelter and safe.

SONIA: I'm not going anywhere, except you know where and I don't mean that place, either.

PETER: You're perfectly well.

SONIA: Well? How dare you say I'm well. I won't last the night – still, it'll make a change.

JASON: Sonia, marry me while there's still time.

SONIA: I would if I could but I can't, because you'll be burying me tomorrow. Being married and being buried is almost the same thing for a woman. I'm going to be a man next time.

JASON: Marry me now.

SONIA: Sorry, darling, I want to go unattached. I'm not taking any chances. Maybe the devil's got designs on me. I'm feeling wonderful; all the pains are gone. If this is death why didn't I have more of it? Jason, no funny stuff, bury me near the gasworks – no, no – cremate me and turn me into an egg-timer – your boiled eggs should only have three minutes, Peter.

JASON: You worked hard enough, Sonia.

PETER: Mother, you won't die. You're not the dying sort. You can't, I won't let you. Who'll cook and take care of me?

SYLVIA: Don't waste your time with her; can't you see she's out of her mind?

SONIA: If you're sensible, thank God I'm mad.

JASON: Sonia, we have witnesses – we could become one here and now.

SONIA: Don't be a dirty old man, you dirty old man.

JASON: Huh, the pot calls the kettle black.

PETER: Shut up.

SONIA: Peter darling, if you are that scared you'd better shelter – and if you're frightened of being alone – take her [points to SYLVIA]. Even she's better than nothing.

PETER: I want to go but I don't want to go without you. I'm torn two ways.

SYLVIA: You heard what she said, take me. I'm your wife, I demand to go.

PETER: Shut up – can't you see my mother's dying? [*To* JASON] And you shut up – you've been robbing me for years. You're not getting your hands on her money also.

JASON: What money?

PETER: The money she's leaving me.

SONIA: Don't be too sure.

JASON: You are a mad crank who's gone balmy, and on top of that you're out of your mind.

SONIA: If they do this today what will they be like tomorrow? Time, gentlemen, please. I'm dying to get some peace.

JASON: I loved her; you ruined everything.

PETER: I love her and from now on I'm finished with you.

SONIA: Have you no respect for the dying?

JASON: When she's dead you can take care of yourself – if you can.

PETER: When she's dead I'm taking over everything. Completely.

SONIA: Listen, I'm not dead yet and what's more – if you go on like this I won't die.

PETER: Don't threaten me.

SONIA: Listen, Peter, you'll have to fend for yourself – a few cooking hints. To make an omelette crack the eggs first, throw them in the pan, and light the gas.

PETER: The bloody world is gonna burst before our very eyes.

JASON: You're mad.

SONIA: When you come to think about it – everyone who made a terrible fortune has been out of their mind – There was the man with motor cars in America and that man who struck it rich with frying oil and my Uncle Sydney.

JASON: Be serious, Sonia.

SONIA: To make a soufflé separate the white from the yellow – whisk the white, fold in the yellow, and in seventeen minutes it's nice and brown and golden.

SYLVIA: Peter, please, we can start all over again – we've got everything down there –

SONIA: Even a swimming pool and a picture palace. [*To 'Beautiful Dreamer'*] Beautiful cheesecake, creamy and rich, tender roast chicken and smoked salmon sandwich. By the way, son, drink a lot of milk.

SYLVIA: What's all her money worth now? You can't buy a visa into heaven.

SONIA: That's what you think. I've just been having a chat with their immigration officers. Nice boys. Peter, do yourself a favour. Buy a yacht – drift over the south seas and buy a few islands – use one island for a living room and another for a bedroom – leave your terrible wife, take Penny with you. I have something to confess, Peter – I loved your father the most.

PETER: Why drag him up? Go to sleep, Mum, you must be tired.

SONIA: No, you go to sleep. I'll sing you a song.

PETER: You'll make me cry. [*Sits by her.*]

SONIA: Why? It's me who's dying. Hush. I'll sing you a going to sleep song. [*She strokes his hair as she sings:*]
When Peter was a little boy, he heard the angels sing;
They flew into the living-room and said 'You will be king.'
'Of what will I be king?' Peter did reply.
'You'll be king of your domain, underneath the sky.'
'Where, oh where, is my domain? Who and where am I?'
'In your heart and in your brain – now go to sleep, my boy.'
When Peter was a little boy, he heard the angels sing;
They flew far from the living-room when they proclaimed him king.
[PETER *is almost asleep, but* SONIA *slumps forward over him.*]

PETER: Help me, oh, she's gone.

SYLVIA: She's at rest now.

JASON: Well, how do you want her buried?

SONIA [*sitting up*]: You soon got over loving me.

JASON: But I thought – oh –

SONIA: I've changed my mind. I don't want to die in the afternoon. Besides I'm thirsty.

JASON: I'll get you some water.

SONIA: Don't be bloody daft, I want wine. I want to be drunk when I go out – drunk and dancing, dancing and singing. I'll show 'em.

PETER: *Who?*

SONIA [*pointing at the sky*]: Those who come and go.

PETER: Listen, everyone, isn't that beautiful? My mother's talking to the angels.

SONIA: They're just like people. Already they've been on the tap talking about partnerships and singing 'Buddy can you spare a diamond'. Where's the wine? [*She stands.*]

PETER: Mother, please don't exert yourself.

JASON: But, Sonia, you're dying – this isn't decent.

SYLVIA: Let her finish it off quick.

SONIA: I'll dance into death – poke out your tongue at the dark and say here's mud in your eye and fluff in your keyhole. [*She dances a few steps, sings:*] Dancing in the dark – Jason, may I have this waltz with you?

JASON: What waltz?

[*She now dances to* PETER *when* JASON *moves away with horror.* PETER *moves backward, also afraid.*]

SONIA: Peter, dance with your mummy.

PETER [*trying to draw her towards the shelter door*]: I'll dance with you downstairs.

SONIA: Who will dance with me? *Who? Who? Who?*

ALEX [*who has moved forward with* PENNY *to watch the proceedings*]: I will.

SONIA: Who are you?

ALEX: A friend of the family.

SONIA: Do you come here often?

ALEX: I live here, over there. Don't you know me? [*He takes her in his arms and they dance.*]

SONIA: Why didn't you come sooner. Have you got some wine?

ALEX: Something better. I've been saving this for a special occasion – Champagne. [*He pretends to pop a bottle and they both drink straight from it.*]

72

SONIA: I name this battleship *Potemkin* – may God forgive me and all who sail in me.

[*Music is heard and they dance round faster and faster.*]

Faster, faster, hold me tight.

PETER [*tries to intervene*]: Stop it. Leave her alone.

SONIA: Faster. Another swig, my lovely man. They're all gone. Just you and me – why did we miss each other? Why did you come too late?

[ALEX *cannot keep up with her and soon she breaks away from him and dances by herself watched by the others who stand around her. She moves tragically and almost drops several times but* ALEX *stands forward and seems to encourage her to move. She smiles and carries on but gradually during the course of this next song she slows right down and stops.*]

Dance before you die, dance into the sky – dance into the dark – do not ask me why – while your legs can move – make the most of them – while your arms can wave – oh wave me away – dance while you still live – live while you're alive – every moment snatch yourself a chance and dance – before you dance into the dance into the – d–a–rk.

[*She stumbles, looks around at* PETER, *and falls dead. Everyone rushes forward and stands round her except* PETER *who moves back;* PENNY *goes to him.*

JASON *blows a whistle.* JOHN *and* JACK *come out and are ready to move her.*]

PETER: Leave her alone.

JASON: I'll handle this. Stand back everyone.

ALEX: So long, old girl, I'll be seeing you.

[JASON *directs the men who bring a little market barrow and wheel her off into his shop.*]

SYLVIA: You're free now – now we can go down.

JASON: I'll handle everything.

SYLVIA: Good – I won't be long – I'll get the valuables. [*She rushes into the shop and frantically sorts out things.*]

PETER: There's no time to lose. [*He sees* PENNY *who is about to push off with* ALEX.] Penny, please, don't go without me.

PENNY: So you're coming then? Good.

PETER: No, you must come with me. I want you. Come, let's go down.

PENNY: No.

PETER: But you love me. You said you did.

PENNY: I do, but I will not come with you. If you give up everything now and come with me we might be happy – but we must leave right now.

PETER: Wait. I can't leave – my mother died here –

ALEX: Come on, Penny – I smell rain – I smell thunder and it looks like a big storm. So long, son, take care of yourself.

PETER: Penny, come back – I love you – Alex, don't leave me.

ALEX: You got what you wanted. Was it worth the price?

PENNY: I loved him – but I waited too long – you understand, don't you?

ALEX: Of course I do – Come on, no more words. [*They go off.*]
   [*As* ALEX *and* PENNY *leave, the people in the factory stop and come outside – the whistle has sounded a tea-break and they smoke and sit quietly staring ahead.*]

TOM: Here, where are you going?
   [PETER *has just decided to go down the shelter and his hand is on the door.* SYLVIA *still frantically tries to pack things.* PETER *pulls back.*]

PETER: Oh bless you – Bless you all – As you know, my dear mother has died and I am going on a little holiday. I'm off to visit our dear dark cousins in the commonwealth of Lambeth and Camden Town – our illustrious history is bound together in a sacred bond – in one broad Superstore of – of prosperity and knowledge – I cherish memories of progress and – er um – that kind of thing – etcetera – etcetera – Work hard and good-bye – [*He waves his hand grandly as the whistle blows. They all still stare at him as he enters the shelter.*]

JASON: Get them back to work. We're wasting time.

JACK [*rushing there*]: Didn't you hear the whistle?

JOHN: Tea-break's over – back to work.

MR BUTCHER: We were watching Mr Mann saying good-bye.

MR FISH: He's going on holiday.

MR GREEN: He's not going, he's gone.

JOHN: Yes, yes, come on then – good-bye, Mr·Mann.

JACK: Wrap up warm. For he's a jolly good fellow –

JOHN: For the sake of Auld Lang Syne. There'll always be an England –

JACK: As long as you are mine.

[JASON *sounds the work whistle again and they all stream back.* JOHN *carries three boxes to* JASON *and* JACK *some ledgers.*]

JASON: Well, he's out of the way. What have you got there?

JOHN: Latest samples. Want to see them?

JASON: In a moment. What's the latest figures?

JACK [*consults book*]: Skegness and Shoreditch working to capacity – 50,000 produced last week. Glasgow, Helsinki, and Camberwell are working day and night on the special Empire Shroud – Whitechapel and Tel Aviv are concentrating on the Kosher for Passover brand –

JASON: Goody, goody!

JACK: Bristol, Birmingham, Bangalore, and Manchester are taking on extra staff, Marseille, Welwyn Garden City, Munich, Amsterdam, Chicago, Lima, and Samarkand simply cannot cope with the orders pouring in.

JASON: In fact, everything in the garden is lovely – Roll on Shroud Tuesday we'll all have some pancakes. Peter Mann may be the richest man in the world, but I'm the richest man on the world. What are we working on here?

JOHN [*undoes the boxes and takes out three shrouds*]: The very latest shroud –

JASON: Of course, designed specially for the Cobalt war – one for Russia, one for America, and one for England.

JOHN: Isn't the world saturated with improved designs?

JACK: Won't they explode the bomb to see if the shrouds work?

JOHN: Isn't the whole economy geared to shrouds?

JASON: You ask too many questions.

[SYLVIA *comes rushing out of the shop, her arms laden with heavy furs and several cases – she is almost bent double with the weight of things hanging from her shoulders. She is dressed in several coats and is over-laden with jewellery. As she rushes she drops many things; each time she tries to pick them up she drops other things – eventually she reaches* JASON, *near the door of the shelter.*]

SYLVIA: Peter! I'm ready, Peter! Where are you? Yoohoo! I've got everything worth while.

JASON: I'm afraid you left it a bit late.

SYLVIA; What do you mean? Where is he? Peter? The door's – shut?

JASON: Yes, and it cannot be opened from the outside and your dear husband is downstairs.

JACK: Singing to spiders –

JOHN: Chattering to rats.

SYLVIA: But I'm his wife – open the door, I've got to join him. What can I do?

JASON: That's your problem, we've got work to do.

SYLVIA: Help me! Help me – I'll be killed. [*She rushes around with panic, trying to hold on to her things.*] Mum, Dad where can I go – help me –

[*The people troop out of the factory.*]

MRS GREEN: What's the matter?

SYLVIA: Mum, help me. Peter's gone.

MR GREEN: Oh yes, Miss Toffeenose, now your old man's run off without you, you come crying back. I told you so.

MRS GREEN: Why didn't he take you on holiday with him?

SYLVIA: He's not on holiday, he's –

JASON: Back to work everyone.

JOHN: Come on, break it up.

JACK: Look lively, get cracking.

TOM: Hold your horses. Where is he?

SYLVIA: He's down below, where I should be – where we should all be – Don't you know – don't any of you realize – The Bomb's gonna explode now. Now! Get that into your thick heads.

MR BUTCHER: The Bomb?

MR FISH: You sure?

[*They start rushing around and trying the door with much fury.*]

MR GREEN: Oh, God!

MRS GREEN: What's he got to do with it?

MRS BUTCHER: What can we do?

MRS FISH: Where can we go?

MR BUTCHER: Where can we hide?

TOM: There's nowhere to hide. We must stick together. Now quiet. Don't let's panic.

JASON: He's right. I assure you nothing will happen and if it does you'll all be protected, adequately.

SYLVIA: Open the door.

ALL: Yes, open the door – let us down – we don't want to die.

TOM: We demand protection, we demand shelter – come on all together – One, two, three, four – who are we dying for? One, two, three, four, five – we want to stay alive. [*They march round and round, this time joined by* SYLVIA.]

SYLVIA: There isn't time – we've had it.

TOM: We're not dead yet.

JOHN [*taking out revolver*]: They soon will be.

JACK: Shall we show them, boss?

JASON: Not that way – Slogans. [*He walks to the marching circle of people.*] Friends, I want someone to make the gesture now – go back to work – I promise you all the best shroud the world has seen –

TOM: Open the door.

JASON: I can't. [*The people continue marching round, and* JASON *and his men stand near shouting slogans.*] Leak-proof shrouds will keep the worm out, keep the body in – they're guaranteed moth-proof!

JOHN		Peter Mann Shrouds, Peter Mann Shrouds,
JASON	[*to 'Jingle Bells'*]	are just the job for you.
JACK		Buy one for your wife and kids, and your pussy too.

JASON: Recommended by the Houseproud Magazine, the Birth Control Centre, and the Death Watch Committee. Ladies and gentlemen – I beg you for your own sakes – you must be protected – We must fight them in the shrouds and on the shrouds; we must never surrender.

TOM: Thought you said there'd be no war.

JASON: I promise you – you can take my word for it and I double-cross my heart – You'll all get a rise – wages are going up on Friday – you have my promise as an undertaker and a gentleman. War? Nobody ordered war – shrouds are to prevent war – I predict peace for a million years.

[*At this moment the sirens start blowing. Everyone freezes.*]

Don't panic! It's a false alarm! [*He takes a transistor radio from his pocket and twiddles with it.*] The radio will confirm it.

[*Atmospherics are first heard, then a calm voice.*]

VOICE: Ladies and gentlemen, the four-minute warning went three minutes ago. Broadcasting will now cease. Good evening!

[*Everyone panics.* MR AND MRS BUTCHER *grab the Red shrouds,* MR AND MRS FISH *grab the Star-Spangled shrouds, and* MR AND MRS GREEN *grab the Union Jack shrouds.*]

MR AND MRS BUTCHER [*sing*]:

The people's shroud is deepest red.
You'll get a shroud when you are dead,
And you, my friend, may kiss my arse,
I have the foreman's job at last.

MR AND MRS FISH [*sing*]:

Oh, say, can you see
My Star-Spangled shroud?
Keep up with the Jones's
And die with the crowd.

MR AND MRS GREEN [*sing*]:

Rule, Britannia,
Britannia rules the shrouds. . . .

[*There is a great searing flash, a rumble, then complete silence. No one is left. A huge enveloping shroud comes down, like a curtain, and covers almost the whole stage. Only the shelter door stands in front of it.*]

PETER [*opens the door, cheerfully peers out*]: Good! It's all over! Where's everyone? Jason! You can all come out – It's all blown over. That's funny, I wonder how long I was down there? [*He sees the shroud.*] What's this? Let me out –

[*A voice like Peter's speaks to him.*]

VOICE: Peeeeet–ter – Peeeet–ter!

PETER: Who's that? Where is everyone?

VOICE: Dead.

PETER: Dead? What do you mean? [*Getting impatient.*] Where's everyone?

VOICE: There's not a person left in the world, just shrouds – shrouds covering the dead world. Want to buy some?

PETER: Then where are their bodies? You're joking.

VOICE: All vaporized – Phufft, nice and hygienic. Well, that's that – that was life –

PETER: What about me?

VOICE: A shadow on a bit of charred earth. Good-bye.

PETER: But there must be people – how can they work if they're not alive? How can we make money and be free and rich?

VOICE: That's your problem and you haven't much time to solve it. 'Bye.

PETER: No! Don't go – We'll split fifty–fifty. I'm afraid.

VOICE: In a few moments you'll die. All sensation will be gone. You'll be a no one with nothing – just like everyone else.

PETER: Come out. I'm not afraid of you. I can't die. I'm starting again. The world's beautiful and it's mine. I can roam the vast deserts – I can fish in the great seas – I can fly through the mountains. This is my earth – I am – invincible – impregnable, invulnerable – I am – feeling sick. [*Reassures himself.*] I've taken my pills, I thought of everything, I'll be all right.

VOICE: You're dying – look at you – crawling about now. You're dying from cancer, from the mushroom of greed and lust and jealousy, apathy, hypocrisy, stupidity, dishonesty.

PETER: That's the way I was born.

VOICE: That's the way you chose to go.

PETER: Penny! Wait for me – Alex! I'll catch you up – come back for me a little way – I'll change – don't go without me. I'll show you, I'll show you all. This little bargain's not all sold out – don't touch me, death – I don't want to die – that's the trouble with this place –

79

The law's always after you. Won't let an honest trader spiel in peace. [*He staggers and falls down.*] What's the matter with me? I can't stand up – no – no – no. Stay away – my eyes are heavy – my legs are heavy – and I'm so cold. I'm falling. . . . Falling down . . . hurtling down, down . . . crashing endlessly through space . . . I feel wonderful . . . free . . . flowering. . . . Let me die with my eyes full of flowers! In the dark a Daffodil might light my way – O Lilac, lull me –

I will float like a Lotus on the endless lake –

O Chrysanthemum – look, I am old – I go to kingdom come – Show me the way. It is night and I grow cold.

I was my enemy – weep for me, Anemone – Mauve, blue, and red. Tulips, touch my lips – for I am dead – lost in the black forests of my head.

ENCLOSE ME, MIMOSA, WITH YOUR SMELL OF ALMONDS.

O, Rose, what river flows by the Lilies-of-the-valley of death?

[*A shape is seen on the other side of the cloth. It comes close to* PETER.]

Let the scent from all the flowers of the world converge on me – All colours merge and sing to me – YES, THEY SING! YES! YES!

Spring – winter – autumn – summer, dance around me and roll into one blazing light –

I enter the flowers. [*He stands up and is ecstatic.*]

I go into the glow of Crocus – INTO THE ETERNAL SKY OF BLUE-BELL – INTO THE BURSTING SUN OF SUNFLOWER AND POPPY – My eyes close – so good-bye Violet – I go to God – if he will have me.

[*He is sprawled on the floor and the figure behind the curtain comes right round and approaches.* PETER *jumps up full of fear.*]

GO AWAY! DON'T TOUCH ME! WHY ME? WHY PICK ON ME? I DON'T WANT TO DIE!

SONIA [*taking off hooded cloak*]: Hello, Peter – I've come for you.

PETER [*falls against her*]: MOTHER! HOW LOVELY YOU LOOK – I thought you were death – I'm cold.

SONIA: Come, Peter – rest now – I'll sing you a song.

PETER: I'm dying.

SONIA: Hush now!

PETER [*he yawns as he lies within her arms*]: Oh – I'm so tired. How glad I was to see you.

SONIA [*sings*]: When Peter was a little boy – he heard the angels sing –

PETER: Help me – don't let me die –

SONIA: He flew into the living-room and said, 'You will be king –'

PETER: Give me another chance – I'll be good.

SONIA: 'Of what will I be king?' Peter did reply. . . .

PETER: You see I know the difference –

SONIA: 'You'll be king of your domain –' Peter be a good boy –

PETER: Mother, hold me.

SONIA [*sings*]: They flew away from his domain when they proclaimed him king.

PETER: Oh, Mother, I'm – dead. [*He slumps across her.*]

[SONIA *leans over* PETER *and the stage goes completely dark. Sparks and stars seem to strike the sky. When the lights come on again the huge shroud has gone, everything is as it was in Act One.* THE DREAM HAS ENDED. SONIA *has gone and it is* ALEX *instead who leans over* PETER *who is lying on the floor of his mother's shop.* SONIA *is with* JASON *celebrating with the others inside the house of Mr and Mrs Butcher. Music is heard from there.*]

ALEX: Wake up! Peter, wake up! [*He slaps* PETER'*s face.*]

[PETER *sits up, holds his head and shakes it, and then stands up and looks dazed.*]

PETER: I'm not dead! Boy, have I been dreaming.

ALEX: Look, let's get the money – let's get going.

[PETER *lifts the safe from the floor and puts it on a chair.*]

Don't you want to go now?

PETER: I'm going –

ALEX: Good. Uranium, Uranium, boom, boom – Get the money, what's the matter with you?

PETER: I'm starting with nothing – that way I've got nothing to lose. It was such a crazy mixed-up dream. You were in it and I destroyed the world.

ALEX: You knocked yourself out.

PETER: Telling me. It all began with me pinching the money. So no money this time. World, here I come! One, two, three, four, five – It's bloody great to be alive. Let's get going before Penny gets back – married. Oh God, she's so beautiful. I was such a stupid fool. I love her, I love her. Why didn't I see it before? Why did I have to wait for a dream to show me?

[*Meanwhile,* PENNY *has entered the street wearing her wedding gown. She looks very unhappy and is followed by* TOM *who holds her bouquet very dejectedly. She leaves* TOM *all alone and leans against the wall of Sonia's shop, where she weeps.* ALEX *slowly puts the safe back on to the shelf, and* PETER *wanders outside and sees* PENNY *who pretends she is not crying.*]

I hope you'll be happy.

PENNY: I hope you'll be happier.

PETER: It's too late now, you're married so that's that.

PENNY: I couldn't go through with it.

PETER: What? Am I awake? [*Pinches himself.*] Pinch me. [*She does.*] Ouch! Just say that again.

PENNY: I couldn't marry Tom. If it's not you, it's not anyone.

PETER: PENNY! I love you. I've been such a swine but I love you.

[*They embrace and kiss and just look at each other. Soon they are dancing round and round to the music from the Butcher's shop. They dance into Sonia's shop and* ALEX *joins the other people who have danced into the street.*]

WOMEN [*seeing* TOM]: They're here!

MEN: They're here.

WOMEN: Three cheers!

MEN: Three cheers!

[*They dance around the dejected* TOM. SONIA *and* JASON *dance together.* ALEX, *greatly admiring* SONIA, *taps* JASON *on shoulder.*]

ALEX: Excuse me. My God, every acre a woman. [SONIA *is flattered as he dances away with her. They dance faster and faster. Then they sway cheek to cheek.*] You're beautiful!

SONIA: I know.

ALEX: You dance divinely.

SONIA: You don't, but you do have a nice shoulder to lean on.

ALEX: Hundreds of women have said that.

SONIA: Stay to dinner.

ALEX: Not enough have said that. You're ravishing.

SONIA: I agree, but I was even more sensational a few years ago.

ALEX: You inspire me. [*He seems to be creating a poem on the spur of the moment.*] WHAT MYSTICAL LIGHT SHINES BETWEEN YOUR EYES – ? COME, LET US WRITE OUR LOVE UPON THE SKIES – LET'S DREAM TILL DOOMSDAY – DRUNK WITH LUSTY WINE – OH, FULL-BLOWN BEAUTY – PASSIONATE – DIVINE.

[*He smiles at her, very pleased with himself, but she suddenly gives him a whack and nearly knocks him off his feet.*]

SONIA: You rat, take that! You wrote that for me, so you said, twenty years ago.

ALEX: *Sonia!* Sonia, forgive me.

SONIA: *Alex!* Only you could shoot such a line and have me believing it twice.

ALEX: Only you could have made me say it twice.

SONIA: Only you could wriggle out of everything. [*He holds her and tries to move her around to the music. She is stubborn at first, but gradually succumbs.*] How we danced! Like a dream. All the cups and competitions we won! We danced like this through the Palais de Danses of Moscow, Paris, and Hammersmith.

ALEX: No, not Hammersmith.

SONIA: That's right. Not Hammersmith! How dare you come back. [*She swipes him again.*]

ALEX: Forgive me! I want to settle down, to turn over a new leaf. [*He tries to kiss her.*]

SONIA: My name's not Eve. [*She acts seductively.*]

ALEX: You're my wife, my lovely wife.

SONIA: You're my husband, my lousy husband. [*She gives him another crack.*]

ALEX: We all make mistakes. Forgive? Sonia, how old are you now?

SONIA: How old do you want me to be?

[*They cuddle and kiss, but* JASON *breaks them up.*]

JASON: Sonia, even though you flirt, I still want to get married to you. The bedspring's been oiled and the bubble's in the wine, so let's get down to business.

SONIA: Sorry. It seems I'm married to this man for better or worse.

JASON: That man? There's no accounting for taste. Well, an undertaker must be practical.

[JASON *goes to* SYLVIA *and pinches her on the bottom.*]

Come here, my dear. Florists and undertakers have a lot in common, they should get together.

[*The market people are still dancing around* TOM, *pelting him with confetti and rice.*]

MRS BUTCHER: Where's my daughter, then?

MRS FISH: Yes, where's the bride?

TOM: It's no good you dancing. She wouldn't go through with it. She's run off after that Peter Mann again.

ALL: Oh dear!

[*Everyone picks up the confetti and rice and then they quickly return to their stalls and get ready for business.* ALEX *and* SONIA *start dancing again, and* PETER *and* PENNY *dance out of the house. The two couples collide.*]

SONIA: My no-good son! Come, let me introduce you to your no-good father.

PETER: You? My dad? That settles it, I'm off.

ALEX: My son? My goodness. And you'd pinch your own mother's money?

PETER: Yeah, who tried to talk me into it?

SONIA: What's that?

ALEX: Oh – nothing – Come here, son. Wanderlust, eh? It's in the blood.

SONIA: If he takes after you I feel sorry for him and sorry for you and I feel sorry for myself. So let's all go inside and live happy ever after.

PETER: No! We're off. We've made up our minds.

PENNY: We love each other and that's all that matters.

84

PETER: And I've learnt a few things. I know what I do want – I want Penny – I know what I don't want – Superstores and Uranium.

MARKET PEOPLE [*sing*]: MONEY IS TIME AND TIME IS MONEY;
IF YOU'RE BROKE IT ISN'T FUNNY – [*Etc.*
They carry on chanting in the background as they work.]

SONIA: Now he runs away. Trust him – you give them everything and this is how they repay you. Kids of today.

ALEX: It's right they should go. Give us a chance for peace and quiet.

PETER: Dad, that's the first sensible thing you've said.

SONIA: Ah, good riddance! And who'll look after you, sonny boy? Her? She's not good enough for you, darling.

MRS BUTCHER: My Penny's fit for a king.

SONIA: Maybe, but not good enough for my Peter.

MRS BUTCHER: They deserve each other, they're both no good.

SONIA: How dare you talk that way about him? They're both wonderful kids. Go, go – with my blessings – all right – think I care? Go – wrap up warm – they drive you mad. Eat well and don't get run over.

PETER: This is it. Ready?

PENNY: Ready when you are.

[*They are about to go when they see the market people working furiously.*]

MARKET PEOPLE: MONEY IS TIME AND TIME IS MONEY,
MIGHT AS WELL DIE IF YOU HAVEN'T ANY –

PETER [*breaks in on them*]:

MONEY IS TIME? AND TIME IS MONEY?
YOU MISERABLE LOT, YOU'RE NOT EVEN FUNNY.
THE GRAVE DEMANDS NO ENTRANCE FEE,
WHY WAIT FOR DEATH TO SET YOU FREE?
SO PRAISE YOUR SWEET ALMIGHTY POUND,
BUT SPEND IT WHILE YOU'RE STILL AROUND. Don't you see – you can always make money, but you can't always make merry. You're saving up for nothing, going nowhere, hoarding nothing, losing – everything – What will YOU bid for LIFE? Here it is. A kiss in the dark. The one and only – all shapes and sizes – lovely, lousy,

terrible, terrific. Magnificent! Ridiculous! But it's the only one we've got. A great opportunity never to be repeated – a unique bargain – going – going – so make the most if it before it's gone!

[*He grabs hold of* PENNY *and the market people seem to be happy – they have stopped work and stand around the couple.*]

PETER: DOCKERS! DOCTORS! SAINTS OR SINNERS!
TAILORS! SAILORS! LOSERS! WINNERS!
SHIRKERS! WORKERS! BANKERS! BROKERS!
MISERS! WHORES! WIDEBOYS OR JOKERS!
MAKE THE MOST OF LIFE BEFORE
YOU ARE NO MORE – YOU ARE NO MORE.

MR BUTCHER: The boy's right!

MR FISH: Absolutely right!

MRS GREEN: Let's give them gifts.

MRS BUTCHER: Let's do them proud.

JASON [*measures Peter*]: I'll send it on.

[TOM *gives them the bouquet of flowers and the market people load them up with gifts as they sing.*]

MR FISH [*sings*]: Don't argue over fish,
There's plenty in the sea;
There's cod for you, skate for you
And Dover Sole for me.

MR GREEN [*sings*]: The earth is very fruitful,
So take this fruit I'm giving.
Oh pardon me, that's half a crown,
I've got to make a living.

Who wants to buy a chicken?
The very best I've got.
Here, take my wife as well!
Ten bob for the lot.

JASON: And don't fight over coffins,
There's plenty to go round.
Personally, I'm getting cremated,
But don't spread that around.

PETER:
We're all in this together,
A dream in endless space,
The earth is but one country,
The world's a market place.

[*Everyone cheers as* PETER *and* PENNY *go off.* SONIA *and* ALEX *go into the house. The market people stop cheering and laughing and go back to work as if their lives depended on it – and chant –*]

MARKET PEOPLE: MONEY IS TIME AND TIME IS MONEY –
MONEY IS TIME AND TIME IS MONEY –
MONEY IS TIME AND TIME IS MONEY –

THE CURTAIN FALLS

FULL VERSIONS OF SONGS

(pages 15 and 16)

> Peach, Plum, or Apricot!
> How much money have you got?
> If you've got a bob or two,
> I will bring some home for you.
>
> Apricot, Peach, or Plum!
> We may get blown to kingdom come,
> Let us eat our fruit before
> Our parents go again to war.
>
> Plum, Apricot, or Peach!
> Hide the stone from out their reach,
> So that it falls into the earth
> And brings another world to birth.
>
> Peach, Plum, or Apricot!
> The world's gone mad, the whole damn lot.
> To hell with them, let's dream and fly,
> There's more in life than meets the eye.

(page 24)

> Uranium, uranium, boom, boom, boom!
> Cling clang, zing zang!
> Boom, womb, ZOOM!
> Get this in your cranium,
> Stuff your old geranium,
> I'm off to get uranium, boom! boom! boom!
>
> Uranium, uranium, boom, boom, boom!
> Bing bang, zing zang!
> Boom, womb, ZOOM!
> I'm a crazy, hazy, zany un,
> A raving stark insanium,
> But I'm off to get uranium, boom! boom! boom!

Uranium, uranium, boom, boom, boom!
Ring rang, zing zang!
Boom, womb, ZOOM!
I've a super manic panium
Inside my super brainium,
And I'm off to get uranium, boom! boom! boom!

(*page 31*)

Money is time and time is money.
Might as well die if you haven't any.
Money makes the world go round.
Oh praise thee, sweet almighty pound.
Money is time and time is money.
If you are broke it isn't funny,
And our love will not grow old,
Provided it is set in gold.
Money is time and time is money.
If you're rich the world is sunny,
For money opens every door.
Give us more and more and more and more.
For money makes the church bells ring –
Oh thank you, God, for everything.

(*page 33*)

Let Jason help you getting wed.
He'll sell you a double bed,
The pills to make your mattress sing,
A hearse, a horse, a diamond ring.
I'll buy a husband just for you,
Or perhaps you'd like a kangaroo.
Life insurance? A samovar?
A Cadillac or caviar?
A virgin parrot newly caught?
Picture postcards? You know the sort.
What you want I bet I've got –
A 'cello or a chamber – orchestra.

I can suit you for a fee,
In the end you'll come to me.
The name is Jason, don't forget –
What you want I can always get.

(page 40)

There's a woman down the road, thought she'd last forever,
So she saved ten thousand pounds for the rainy weather,
But now she's dead, yes, now she's dead,
The worms are chewing through her head,
In the rainy wea–ther.

There's a geezer down the lane, had fifty thousand nicker,
But he couldn't find a cure for his wonky ticker.
The money's saved but he is dead,
The worms are breeding in his head,
Gobbling up his tic–ker.

There's a broker lived up West, had no time for eating.
Made a fortune out of foam, the kind they use for seating.
He got so rich and got so thin,
The worms will make quick work of him,
Eating up his sea–ting.

(page 40)

Oh, the walls are thin in London Town,
They wouldn't need much blowing down.
So workers of the world unite,
Before we vanish in the night.

My dreams are thin and wearing thinner,
No one expects me home for dinner.
Oh, comrades of the universe,
There's nothing better but plenty worse.

The streets are cold in London Town,
No one smiles, all look down.
Where are our dreams of liberty?
Oh, what became of you and me?

The streets are full with empty eyes,
Oh, workers of the world arise.
Can't you hear the sirens call?
Comrade death unites us all.

We're all together on the rocks,
A crawling lot of crooked crocks,
Just one chance in eternity.
Oh, shake your chains and dream you're free.

(page 63)

Put up the banns, pull down the blinds,
For my darling you are mine.
Don't let's wait, I can't last forever,
Take the plunge, it's either now or never.
Rush up the stairs, better say your prayers,
I've got that twinkle in my eye.
We'll make love, the loveliest, the longest,
And we'll fight to see who is the strongest.
Come over here or I'll come over there
Watch out for my adrenaline.
Jump into bed, good-bye maidenhead.
Tonight you will be really mine.
Put out the light, here goes, so hold me tight,
We're going to have a smashing time.

(page 71)

When Peter was a little boy, he watched the angels fly,
Around him in the garden, where the clothes hang out to dry.
They sang to him of heaven, a hymn of hope and joy.
'Oh, bring it down to earth,' he said – 'why hide it in the sky?'

When Peter was a little boy, he heard the angels sing;
They flew into the living-room and said, 'You will be king.'
'Of what will I be king?' Peter did reply.
'You'll be king of your domain, underneath the sky.'
'Where, oh where, is my domain? Who and where am I?'
'In your heart and in your brain – now go to sleep, my boy.'

When Peter was a little boy, he heard the angels sing;
They flew far from the living-room when they proclaimed him
    king.